BARBARA WALTERS

WOMEN of ACHIEVEMENT

BARBARA WALTERS

Henna Remstein

CHELSEA HOUSE PUBLISHERS
PHILADELPHIA

Chelsea House Publishers
EDITOR IN CHIEF Stephen Reginald
PRODUCTION MANAGER Pamela Loos
ART DIRECTOR Sara Davis
MANAGING EDITOR James D. Gallagher
PHOTO EDITOR Judy L. Hasday
SENIOR PRODUCTION EDITOR Lisa Chippendale

Staff for **Barbara Walters**
SENIOR EDITOR Therese De Angelis
ASSOCIATE ART DIRECTOR Takeshi Takahashi
PICTURE RESEARCHER Patricia Burns
DESIGNER Brian Wible
COVER DESIGN Takeshi Takahashi

3 5 7 9 8 6 4 2

Library of Congress Cataloging-in-Publication Data

Remstein, Henna, 1968-
Barbara Walters / by Henna Remstein.
104 pp.   cm. — (Women of achievement)
Includes bibliographical references and index.
Summary: A biography of the television journalist whose interviewing skills
have won her seven Emmy Awards in her thirty-year career.
ISBN 0-7910-4716-4 (hc). — ISBN 0-7910-4717-2 (pbk).

1. Walters, Barbara, 1931-   —Juvenile literature. 2. Television journalists—
United States—Biography—Juvenile literature. 3. Television personalities—
United States—Biography—Juvenile literature. I. Title. II. Series.
PN4874.W285R46 1998
363.7—dc21
[B]   98-2789
                                                                   CIP
                                                                    AC

Cover Photo: *Photofest*

Frontis: Barbara Walters on
the set of her anniversary
special in 1996.

CONTENTS

WOMEN of ACHIEVEMENT

Jane Addams
SOCIAL WORKER

Madeleine Albright
STATESWOMAN

Marian Anderson
SINGER

Susan B. Anthony
WOMAN SUFFRAGIST

Clara Barton
AMERICAN RED CROSS FOUNDER

Margaret Bourke-White
PHOTOGRAPHER

Rachel Carson
BIOLOGIST AND AUTHOR

Cher
SINGER AND ACTRESS

Hillary Rodham Clinton
FIRST LADY AND ATTORNEY

Katie Couric
JOURNALIST

Diana, Princess of Wales
HUMANITARIAN

Emily Dickinson
POET

Elizabeth Dole
POLITICIAN

Amelia Earhart
AVIATOR

Gloria Estefan
SINGER

Jodie Foster
ACTRESS AND DIRECTOR

Betty Friedan
FEMINIST

Althea Gibson
TENNIS CHAMPION

Ruth Bader Ginsburg
SUPREME COURT JUSTICE

Helen Hayes
ACTRESS

Katharine Hepburn
ACTRESS

Mahalia Jackson
GOSPEL SINGER

Helen Keller
HUMANITARIAN

**Ann Landers/
Abigail Van Buren**
COLUMNISTS

Barbara McClintock
BIOLOGIST

Margaret Mead
ANTHROPOLOGIST

Edna St. Vincent Millay
POET

Julia Morgan
ARCHITECT

Toni Morrison
AUTHOR

Grandma Moses
PAINTER

Lucretia Mott
WOMAN SUFFRAGIST

Sandra Day O'Connor
SUPREME COURT JUSTICE

Rosie O'Donnell
ENTERTAINER AND COMEDIAN

Georgia O'Keeffe
PAINTER

Eleanor Roosevelt
DIPLOMAT AND HUMANITARIAN

Wilma Rudolph
CHAMPION ATHLETE

Elizabeth Cady Stanton
WOMAN SUFFRAGIST

Harriet Beecher Stowe
AUTHOR AND ABOLITIONIST

Barbra Streisand
ENTERTAINER

Elizabeth Taylor
ACTRESS AND ACTIVIST

Mother Teresa
HUMANITARIAN AND
RELIGIOUS LEADER

Barbara Walters
JOURNALIST

Edith Wharton
AUTHOR

Phyllis Wheatley
POET

Oprah Winfrey
ENTERTAINER

Babe Didrikson Zaharias
CHAMPION ATHLETE

"REMEMBER THE LADIES"

MATINA S. HORNER

"Remember the Ladies." That is what Abigail Adams wrote to her husband John, then a delegate to the Continental Congress, as the Founding Fathers met in Philadelphia to form a new nation in March of 1776. "Be more generous and favorable to them than your ancestors. Do not put such limited power in the hands of the Husbands. If particular care and attention is not paid to the Ladies," Abigail Adams warned, "we are determined to foment a Rebellion, and will not hold ourselves bound by any Laws in which we have no voice, or Representation."

The words of Abigail Adams, one of the earliest American advocates of women's rights, were prophetic. Because when we have not "remembered the ladies," they have, by their words and deeds, reminded us so forcefully of the omission that we cannot fail to remember them. For the history of American women is as interesting and varied as the history of our nation as a whole. American women have played an integral part in founding, settling, and building our country. Some we remember as remarkable women who—against great odds—achieved distinction in the public arena: Anne Hutchinson, who in the 17th century became a charismatic religious leader; Phillis Wheatley, an 18th-century black slave who became a poet; Susan B. Anthony, whose name is synonymous with the 19th-century women's rights movement, and who led the struggle to enfranchise women; and in the 20th century, Amelia Earhart, the first woman to cross the Atlantic Ocean by air.

These extraordinary women certainly merit our admiration, but other women, "common women," many of them all but forgotten, should also be recognized for their contributions to American thought and culture. Women have been community builders; they have founded schools and formed voluntary associations to help those in need; they have assumed the major responsibility for rearing children, passing on from one generation to the next the values that keep a culture alive. These and innumerable other contributions, once ignored, are now being recognized by scholars, students, and the public. It is exciting and gratifying that a part of our history that was hardly acknowledged a few generations ago is now being studied and brought to light.

In recent decades, the field of women's history has grown from obscurity to a politically controversial splinter movement to academic respectability, in many cases mainstreamed into such traditional disciplines as history, economics, and psychology. Scholars of women, both female and male, have organized research centers at such prestigious institutions as Wellesley College, Stanford University, and the University of California. Other notable centers for women's studies are the Center for the American Woman and Politics at the Eagleton Institute of Politics at Rutgers University; the Henry A. Murray Research Center for the Study of Lives, at Radcliffe College; and the Women's Research and Education Institute, the research arm of the Congressional Caucus on Women's Issues. Other scholars and public figures have established archives and libraries, such as the Schlesinger Library on the History of Women in America, at Radcliffe College, and the Sophia Smith Collection, at Smith College, to collect and preserve the written and tangible legacies of women.

From the initial donation of the Women's Rights Collection in 1943, the Schlesinger Library grew to encompass vast collections documenting the manifold accomplishments of American women. Simultaneously, the women's movement in general and the academic discipline of women's studies in particular also began with a narrow definition and gradually expanded their mandate. Early causes, such as woman suffrage and social reform, abolition, and organized labor were joined by newer concerns, such as the history of women in business and the professions and in politics and government; the study of the family; and social issues such as health policy and education.

Women, as historian Arthur M. Schlesinger Jr., once pointed out, "have constituted the most spectacular casualty of traditional history. They have made up at least half the human race, but you could never tell that by looking at the books historians write." The new breed of historians is remedying that omission. They have written books about immigrant women and about working-class women who struggled for survival in cities and about black women who met the challenges of life in rural areas. They are telling the stories of women who, despite the barriers of tradition and economics, became lawyers and doctors and public figures.

The women's studies movement has also led scholars to question traditional interpretations of their respective disciplines. For example, the study of war has traditionally been an exercise in military and political analysis, an examination of strategies planned and executed by men. But scholars of women's history have pointed out that wars have also been periods of tremendous change and even opportunity for women, because the very absence of men on the home front enabled them to expand their educational, economic, and professional activities and to assume leadership in their homes.

The early scholars of women's history showed a unique brand of courage in choosing to investigate new subjects and take new approaches to old ones. Often, like their subjects, they endured criticism and even ostracism by their academic colleagues. But their efforts have unquestionably been worthwhile, because with the publication of each new study and book another piece of the historical patchwork is sewn into place, revealing an increasingly comprehensive picture of the role of women in our rich and varied history.

Such books on groups of women are essential, but books that focus on the lives of individuals are equally indispensable. Biographies can be inspirational, offering their readers the example of people with vision who have looked outside themselves for their goals and have often struggled against great obstacles to achieve them. Marian Anderson, for instance, had to overcome racial bigotry in order to perfect her art and perform as a concert singer. Isadora Duncan defied the rules of classical dance to find true artistic freedom. Jane Addams had to break down society's notions of the proper role for women in order to create new social situations, notably the settlement house. All of these women had to come to terms both with themselves and with the world in which they lived. Only then could they move ahead as pioneers in their chosen callings.

Biography can inspire not only by adulation but also by realism. It helps us to see not only the qualities in others that we hope to emulate, but also, perhaps, the weaknesses that made them "human." By helping us identify with the subject on a more personal level they help us feel that we, too, can achieve such goals. We read about Eleanor Roosevelt, for instance, who occupied a unique and seemingly enviable position as the wife of the president. Yet we can sympathize with her inner dilemma; an inherently shy woman, she had to force herself to live a most public life in order to use her position to benefit others. We may not be able to imagine ourselves having the immense poetic talent of Emily Dickinson, but from her story we can understand the challenges faced by a creative woman who was expected to fulfill many family responsibilities. And though few of us will ever reach the level of athletic accomplishment displayed by Wilma Rudolph or Babe Zaharias, we can still appreciate their spirit, their overwhelming will to excel.

A biography is a multifaceted lens. It is first of all a magnification, the intimate examination of one particular life. But at the same time, it is a wide-angle lens, informing us about the world in which the subject lived. We come away from reading about one life knowing more about the social, political, and economic fabric of the time. It is for this reason, perhaps, that the great New England essayist Ralph Waldo Emerson wrote in 1841, "There is properly no history: only biography." And it is also why biography, and particularly women's biography, will continue to fascinate writers and readers alike.

On May 1, 1996, Barbara Walters hosted what she called a "personal memoir" of
her 20 years with ABC.

1

AS FAMOUS AS
HER SUBJECTS

On the morning of September 6, 1997, throngs of mourners lined the streets of London, England, braced for the funeral procession of Princess Diana, who had died in a devastating car accident the previous Sunday. Perched above the crowds in a sound box, Barbara Walters narrated the day's events with her ABC colleague Peter Jennings and interviewed many of the people who had known, admired, and loved Diana Spencer. The previous night, on a special 20/20 program entitled "The Last Farewell," Walters had talked at length with pop singer Elton John about his longtime friendship with Diana. As few interviewers could, Walters asked the star to share his grief and to speak about his role in the upcoming memorial service at Westminster Abbey.

At 66 years old, with more than 30 years of experience, Barbara Walters was a natural choice to cover an event with profound, worldwide repercussions. As a seasoned journalist and poised interviewer, she reported each sobering moment with a sense that she too felt the magnitude of such a great loss.

This was not the first funeral of a world figure that Walters had covered. In 1981, she traveled to the Middle East twice in one week to report on the deaths of two men who had been friends, Egyptian president Anwar Sadat and Israeli politician Moshe Dayan. Yet for many Americans, Walters's role as commentator at Diana Spencer's funeral may have seemed out of the ordinary. Since the late 1970s, she had become primarily identified as a celebrity interviewer, the force behind the eponymous *Barbara Walters Special.*

While walking arm in arm through the woods or sitting in a posh living room, on a movie set, or in a cold-tiled jail cell, Barbara Walters talks with the famous and the infamous about their lives and their families, their dreams and their heartbreaks, their pasts and their futures. Eliciting stories and memories—and frequently a few tears—from her subjects has become her trademark. She gets the scoop. The networks bank on her to generate reliable ratings, and legions of fans tune in to hear her ask questions that they wish they could ask themselves. Her allegiance is with the viewer; her specialty is the one-on-one chat. Decades of taking on groundbreaking interviews have made Barbara Walters as celebrated as her subjects.

The names of those subjects merely hint at the roster of celebrities, public figures, and newsmakers who have entrusted Barbara Walters with their private lives under the watchful gaze of the nation's television viewers: every president and first lady since the Johnsons; world leaders Menachem Begin, Anwar Sadat, Fidel Castro, and Muammar Gadhafi; public figures in distress like boxer Mike Tyson, tennis pro Monica Seles, and former White House press secretary James Brady; actors Margot Kidder and Christopher Reeve; larger-than-life figures like actors John Wayne and Katherine Hepburn, musician John Lennon, and actor/dancer Fred Astaire. She has also interviewed notorious figures such as Jean Harris, the Menendez brothers, Claus von Bulow, Patty Hearst, and Amy Grossberg, and newsmakers Robert

General Colin Powell, former chairman of the Joint Chiefs of Staff, visits his childhood neighborhood in the Bronx with Barbara Walters in August 1995. Walters had landed the first formal interview with Powell following his retirement.

Shapiro, Louis Farrakhan, Rupert Murdoch, Gloria Steinem, Ivana Trump, and Colin Powell. Walters has spoken with the famously reclusive singer Barbra Streisand, basketball legend Julius Erving, and Olympic medalist Greg Louganis, as well as television and film personalities like Candace Bergen, Annette Bening, Kirk Douglas, Stephen Spielberg, and Lauren Bacall.

On the May 1, 1996, episode of her TV special, Walters promised viewers "some of the best and the worst moments" of her 20-year career with ABC—a career that included a painful stint as coanchor of the *ABC Evening News* as well as scores of dazzling interviews with rock icons, Hollywood legends, and powerful world leaders. The 90-minute retrospective

Walters won the first of seven Emmy Awards in 1975 for her work on NBC's Today *show.*

reviewed the pioneering interviews and innovative reporting that made Walters a leader in broadcast journalism.

Walters and her producers culled a wide sampling of the interviews and news stories she covered during her career at the network. Among the highlights were her groundbreaking 1977 interview with Anwar Sadat and Israeli prime minister Menachem Begin, her momentous Jeep ride with Fidel Castro over rugged Cuban roads, and the now-legendary moment when she asked Katherine Hepburn, "If you were a tree, what kind of tree would you be?" (An oak, replied her subject.) Also featured was Walters's White House interview with first lady Hillary Rodham Clinton—along with Barbara's admission that she should have asked tougher questions. And while the show celebrated Walters's award-winning journalism, it did not shy away from the more controversial moments in her career. During a clip of her interview with president-elect Jimmy Carter, which she ended with the highly criticized plea that he "be wise with us, Governor, be good to us," a self-deprecating Walters asks in a voice-over, "Why couldn't I leave well enough alone?" Indeed, the qualities that are most apparent in the special are Walters's humor and passion for her work, evident in her closing sentiment about TV journalism: "With the grace of God and a good lighting director, I look forward to doing it for a long time."

In many ways, Barbara Walters's approach to interviewing is traditional. Every interview, after all, has a beginning, a middle, and an end. But Barbara manages to conduct interviews with a balanced and informed intensity that nearly always draws out her subjects and convinces them to say more than they thought they might. With Amy Grossberg, for example, a young woman accused of killing her newborn baby, Walters took on the benevolence of a grandmother, asking about the vicious character assessments of Grossberg and her boyfriend that had been reported by the media. She seemed to be a sympathetic friend with Christopher and Dana Reeve when emotions overflowed in their first television interview after Reeve's tragic riding accident. She hit hard with prosecution attorney Christopher Darden in a bluntly delivered statement: "O. J. [Simpson] called you a punk." Because of her reputation for being direct, some subjects approach her interviews as a chance to clear the record or to express an opinion that would otherwise be left unsaid.

Walters appears to be everywhere, not just on current prime-time specials and ABC's twice-weekly *20/20* news show but also on the Lifetime cable network, which has begun running twice each week a selection of her most notable interviews to coincide with the airing of the 60th *Barbara Walters Special.* She is also coanchor of *Turning Point,* another successful ABC newsmagazine show, and anchors the network's annual yearend program, "The Ten Most Fascinating People," first shown in 1994.

Her technique, as she describes it, sounds simple. "I ask everybody: 'If you could interview [Ronald] Reagan, [Richard] Nixon, [Henry] Kissinger, what would you want to know?' A lot of journalists ask the esoteric questions that make them look smart. . . . I want to know what *everybody* wants to know." She writes out her questions—an average of 250 per interview—on index cards and arranges them according to how she plans to conduct the interview. She often begins her interviews with questions about the subject's childhood because generally "that's not only safe for people but opens up all kinds of memories." But the results of her thorough research, probing questions, and basic charm are anything but simple. The seven Emmy Awards decorating her 10th-floor office in the ABC Building in

Manhattan are testaments to her talent and drive and to the reputation she has earned in her field.

Many interviewees attest to her fairness and intelligence. As the star of the TV series *Moonlighting* in 1986, Cybill Shepherd sat with Walters one morning for a conversation that Shepherd found "one of the most interesting interviews I've ever done." A decade later, film actress Sharon Stone recalled with admiration her interview with Barbara for the 1996 pre-Oscar Awards special: "She's intelligent, informed, and charismatic," Stone said. She continued:

> Her own vulnerability and charisma allow you to be vulnerable with her. She's not trying to get some preconceived notion of what she wants in an interview. . . . She goes into the interview with good and informed questions. She's not interested in burning you, but relentlessly searches for something new.

Many observers believe that in her interviews Barbara Walters walks the delicate line between journalism and tabloid gossip. Perhaps there is some truth to this view: to Walters, biography is history, news, and entertainment.

Like many of the public figures she spotlights, Walters has been involved in controversy herself. Actress Angela Lansbury vocally denounced Barbara's invasive questions regarding Lansbury's children and their drug problems. On several other occasions, Walters drew criticism for overstepping the bounds of media ethics by apparently misinterpreting her role as a journalist. In 1986, for example, she delivered confidential papers to the White House in the midst of the Iran-Contra scandal and was censured for acting as a messenger for a government agency. In 1996, she again raised eyebrows after she landed a rare interview with British playwright Andrew Lloyd Webber. The public later learned that Walters had invested $100,000 in Webber's Broadway production of *Sunset Boulevard*. Critics suggested that

her investment had lured Webber or that the connection had at least made him more open to her persuasion. Though Walters did note that Disney, the parent company of ABC, was a major investor in the play, she had not reported her own involvement. After much publicity, she admitted in March 1997 that she "should have disclosed the investment" and promised, "It won't happen again."

Through good and bad publicity, Walters has survived 30 years in a highly capricious industry, where many journalists fear that they are only as successful as their last story. In a 1996 article for *TV Guide*, Walters remembered how lonely she was when she arrived at ABC in 1976, on the eve of her first broadcast as coanchor of the *Evening News*. She had landed not only the

Walters frequently receives tributes for her "tough-minded, intimate" interviewing style and her accomplishments in broadcasting. Here she poses with actress Sharon Stone during the 1994 New York Friars Club dinner, which was held in Walters's honor.

first full-time news anchor position in television history but also the highest salary ever offered to a TV anchor, male or female. "I can barely remember another woman in the newsroom," she recalled, "and I sure could have used a 'sister.'"

Her million-dollar contract turned into a bittersweet victory, however; prestige and power were followed by a firestorm of criticism and controversy. Critics and colleagues questioned Walters's skills and cited her lack of experience in broadcast journalism, while her rising celebrity status alarmed those who questioned her commitment to the tradition and integrity of news. Was she a newsperson or an entertainer? they asked. And either way, was she worth a million dollars?

The critics seemed to discount the years of hard work that had earned Barbara Walters this opportunity. She had been "paying her dues" for more than 16 years by the time she took her place behind the *Evening News* anchor desk with Harry Reasoner on October 4, 1976. She was hired by ABC in 1960 as a writer for the *Today* show, during an era when network executives were likely to have, at most, one female staff member working in their offices. At the time, the only opportunities for women to enter the field occurred when that one female staffer quit, married and left the job, or died.

In this atmosphere, however, the smart, determined, and willful Barbara Walters thrived. From her beginning as a staff writer relegated to working on light human-interest and women's-interest stories, Walters has become the reigning queen of television news: a 1982 Gallup poll named her one of the ten most admired women in the world.

Barbara was born into show business. She grew up amid the glitter of a famous chain of nightclubs owned by her father, Lou Walters. At the Latin Quarter nightclubs, popular singers and comedians and beautiful showgirls entertained crowds of people in the decades before the advent of television drew them back into their own living rooms. In Boston, New York, and Miami, Barbara and her family floated in and out of celebrity circles and high society, depending on the financial status of her father's businesses and on the extent of his gambling debts. Speaking about her childhood with gossip columnist Liz Smith in 1984, Barbara recalled the family's financial ups and downs. "We were rich on Monday and we'd lose it all on Tuesday," she told Smith. "It was not an easy life. It was a life of great splendor and then nothing." A firsthand witness to this roller-coaster life, Barbara learned early lessons in self-sufficiency and the value of education.

Viewers who watched Barbara Walters describing the funeral of Princess Diana that September morning in 1997 did not think about Walters's years of broadcast experience. They were naturally focused on the poignant scenes of the procession, the memorial service in London's Westminster Abbey, and the heartrending sight of Diana's children and other family members following her casket. Yet it was Walters who was able to bring the event into millions of American homes with her sympathetic and informed reporting.

To those who look back at Barbara Walters's career path, it seems inevitable that she would become a news icon and her interviews would become television events. She is one of the most famous interviewers in the world, a "diva" of broadcast journalism. Along the way, her detractors have called her too aggressive or too soft, too feminine or not feminine enough, but no one can ignore her stellar and growing list of accomplishments. She continues to receive high honors for what the *New York Times* called her "toughminded, intimate" style. "Ms. Walters always manages to extract from her subjects at least a few things they never meant to say," the *Times* reported in 1996. "People love her or hate her." Whatever critics and viewers think of Barbara Walters, she is impossible to ignore.

Barbara Walters at the start of her career in broadcasting.

2

"EXTREMELY BRIGHT BUT VERY INTROVERTED"

Barbara Jill Walters was born on September 25, 1929, to Lou and Dena Walters. Barbara's arrival was a happy event for the Walterses, who had experienced a great deal of sadness in the years preceding her birth. Their firstborn, a son named Burton, had died of pneumonia around Christmas 1922, shortly after his first birthday. Four years later, Dena Walters gave birth to a daughter, Jacqueline, who was later diagnosed as mentally handicapped. Three years later, Barbara arrived (most biographical sources incorrectly report the year of her birth as 1931). Though the Walterses loved their children equally and completely, Jacqueline would require a greater portion of their attention and energy. Barbara was often left to entertain herself and sometimes felt like she was on the fringes of her own family.

Lou Walters was born in London, England, to a working-class family. He started his career as an office boy in a vaudeville booking agency in Boston, Massachusetts. A keen business sense and a winning way with people of all kinds brought him success, and he began booking his own acts by the time he was 17. In 1919, when he met his future wife, Dena Seletsky, the granddaughter of

An original program cover for Lou Walters's New York Latin Quarter. The capricious business of owning a nightclub chain meant numerous uprootings and occasional financial setbacks for the Walters family. Nevertheless, Barbara credits her show-business upbringing with having given her the poise and confidence she needed to become a skilled interviewer.

Russian-Jewish immigrants, the 25-year-old was about to open his own booking agency. With his last 75 dollars, he became his own employer, just a few months before marrying his sweetheart. Dena's relatives warmly welcomed the young businessman into their family.

America was in the midst of the "roaring twenties," a period of great prosperity, and the celebratory tone of the country brought business pouring into the Lou Walters Booking Agency. He quickly rose to the top of his field by representing a well-known assortment of variety acts. But this good fortune also allowed him to indulge his passion for gambling, an unfortunate habit that would periodically result in financial difficulty.

When Barbara was very young, the Walterses lived in an expansive 18-room house in Newton, Massachusetts. By the time Barbara turned four, however, Lou's fortunes had vaporized in the wake of the Great Depression, several mistimed investments in the stock market, and the decline of the popularity of vaudeville. Bankruptcy forced him to close his office, sell the house and its furnishings, and struggle through an assortment of odd jobs to feed his family.

But Lou Walters recovered only a few years later, when he not only reopened his booking business but also moved a step closer to reaching his ultimate goal: running a nightclub. He worked out a deal with a friend in which he agreed to assume management of the Cascades Roof, a cabaret atop the Bradford Hotel in Boston. This venture put him "in the black" once again. Buoyed by this success, and with replenished capital, Lou opened what would become a legendary Boston nightclub—the Latin Quarter. The club was an exotic place known for its extravagant decor, an abundance of beautiful showgirls, and headline acts featuring some of the most popular performers of the time, including Milton Berle, Mickey Rooney, Sophie Tucker, Frank Sinatra, and Patti Page.

Newfound wealth signaled another move for the

Brookline, Massachusetts, in the 1930s. Barbara attended Lawrence Elementary School here until the family moved again in 1940.

Walters family, this time into a middle-class Jewish neighborhood in Brookline, a suburb of Boston. There Barbara attended Lawrence Elementary School with the children of aspiring young professionals. Barbara was embarrassed by her father's occupation; for years she lied about the nature of his business and about her parents' friends, many of whom were notable patrons of the club, such as actor Maurice Chevalier, billionaire Howard Hughes, and comedian Chico Marx of the Marx Brothers. Despite the glamour of her father's profession, Barbara wished that her father were a doctor or lawyer instead. (Not until years later, as a young reporter, did Barbara feel that she had benefited from growing up among the celebrated and the elite: during star-struck moments with famous subjects, Walters the interviewer never faltered. Having grown up around such celebrities, she was immediately at ease with them.)

At school, Barbara mostly kept to herself. At the end of each day, she conscientiously did her homework while sitting backstage at the Latin Quarter. Walters also spent a good deal of time at the club helping with daily operations, while her elder sister, Jacqueline, played in quiet contentment in the back office. Barbara and her mother remained close throughout their lives. Even later, during her busiest years and from the farthest corners of the world, Barbara would call Dena several times a week. In contrast, Lou was often absent from his family, making appearances at home on special occasions or religious holidays, although in his old age he and Barbara did develop a closer relationship than they had had while she was growing up.

Each summer, Lou produced his trademark shows at Cape Cod, Massachusetts, while the two girls enjoyed a rural experience at Camp Ferosdel in the Berkshire Hills. A retreat predominantly for Jewish youngsters, the camp provided a quiet, creative atmosphere filled with games, crafts, and nightly campfires. One summer, the lonely Barbara forged a lifelong friendship with another girl at the camp who also had a handicapped sister. The two children were drawn to each other's heightened sense of responsibility and anxiety about her sister's disabilities. The friendship marked a rare period in Barbara's life when she felt comfortable openly admitting to having conflicting feelings about her sister, who required more attention from her parents than she did. She kept this part of her life so private that years later, many of Barbara's adult friends expressed surprise upon learning that Barbara had a mentally disabled sister.

At age 11, on the brink of an awkward adolescence, Barbara found herself uprooted once more from the stable and somewhat sheltered life she was accustomed to. That year, Lou Walters moved the family to sparsely populated Palm Island, off the coast of Miami, Florida, where he was preparing to open his second nightclub.

Next door to the club the Walterses settled in a large and elegantly appointed home. Except for Barbara and Jacqueline, no children lived on the island, so Barbara traveled across Biscayne Bay to the private Iva M. Fisher School, arriving each morning in a chauffeur-driven car. As a newcomer, Barbara found it difficult to make friends with the other children at the school, many of whom had similarly nomadic family lives. While most of her free time during the day was spent alone, except for the company of her dog, her evenings were filled with the adult dazzle of the Latin Quarter and its glamorous patrons.

Barbara's sense of isolation ended in 1942, when Lou Walters again transplanted the family to New York City, the site of his third Latin Quarter. Like its predecessors, the New York club became a regular meeting place of the local cosmopolitan set. With the financial boon that accompanied its success, Lou acquired an apartment overlooking Central Park and enrolled Barbara in the eighth-grade class of the exclusive Fieldston School in the Bronx.

Fieldston School embodied the ideals of private, elite education. The school's small classes and personalized attention catered to a wealthy, sophisticated, and primarily Jewish student body. Barbara enjoyed both the academic prestige and an accepting social circle of savvy city girls. Like her new friends, she soon began shopping at New York's most exclusive department stores, Saks Fifth Avenue and Lord & Taylor, and developed interests common to many teenage girls of the time—makeup, clothes, and boys. For the first time, she felt that she was truly part of a group of her peers.

The Fieldston girls reveled in the freedom of riding the subways on outings to the movies, museums, and stores, and they often rode their bikes together through Central Park. (Barbara's relish for bicycling was evident years later, when she produced a *Today* show segment on the pleasures of peddling through the park, an

Dena, Lou, and Jackie Walters at Lou's Miami Latin Quarter nightclub during the 1940s.

urban experience unfamiliar to most Americans.)

Yet even with such carefree occupations, Barbara indulged in prophetic musings about a career in show business and took great interest in learning the technical aspects of staging and lighting at the New York Latin Quarter. Today, with more than 50 *Barbara Walters Special*s and thousands of news stories to her credit, Walters still contributes to every aspect of her pieces, from camera work to lighting to post-production editing.

Expanding the Miami Latin Quarter club meant uprooting the Walters family for a third time and returning to the very place where Barbara had once felt isolated. This time leaving was even more difficult

An aerial view of the Miami Beach area in the 1940s. Having lived in the area several years earlier, Barbara did not relish another stay there when her father moved the family to expand his nightclub there around 1944.

because she left behind a typical teenage life that she already knew was unattainable on Palm Island. Because America was at war, the United States Army had taken over the family's former house on the island, and the Walters family settled instead in a quiet neighborhood in Miami Beach. Barbara hoped that Miami Beach might make her feel less alienated, but that was not the case. Classmates at Miami Beach Junior High were not accepting of "interlopers" from the North, whom they labeled "snowbirds" after the practice of traveling south each winter to avoid cold weather.

By the 10th grade, Barbara had resolved to change her lot and saw sorority life as a path to popularity. In a brief period, she not only pledged the Lambda Pi sorority but also experienced her first crush and started dating. It didn't last—the Boston Latin Quarter closed and the New York club needed her father's full-time attention. The family returned to the Big Apple shortly after.

For the next few years, the failure of various ill-managed business ventures and gambling debts stripped Lou Walters of his remaining collateral. The subsequent hard times would not be the last for the Walters family. Barbara, then and now a pragmatist, acknowledged thinking that one day she might become the sole financial support for her mother and sister.

With the help of press agents, positive reviews by Broadway columnists, and weekly advertisements in local newspapers, Lou managed to resuscitate the New York club. Now Barbara's parents were away from home more than ever as their business and social lives became more hectic. Barbara usually saw them only briefly each morning. With their increased income, however, Lou and Dena Walters could once again afford to send their daughter to an exclusive school.

Barbara was accepted into the 1947 class of the private, genteel Birch Wathen, known for preparing its affluent students for Ivy League or Seven Sisters colleges. Because of the publicity blitz for the Latin Quarter, Lou Walter's business became public knowledge at the school, much to Barbara's dismay. Rumors traveled among the students, and the school paper, the *Birch Bark*, published a parody of her that was meant to be lighthearted. It nonetheless stung Barbara so sharply that she would later dissociate herself from her alma mater, refusing invitations to speak there or to participate in alumni events.

In spite of the ribbing, however, Barbara participated in extracurricular activities, including working on the school's literary magazine, *Birch Leaves*, where she showed her aptitude for creative writing. Renewed friendships with old classmates from Fieldston filled the remainder of her social calendar. Among classmates at Birch Wathen she remained aloof, though. One classmate remembered her as "extremely bright but very introverted. She made no effort to be friendly." Barbara did put tremendous effort into emulating and even outdoing the fashions of her fellow students, and she is still known for her stand-out wardrobe, both on air and in her private life.

Smart and ambitious, Barbara did well academically at Birch Wathen. Her high school yearbook quote, an arcane citation from the 17th-century English poet Francis Quarles, revealed her serious nature and foretold the foundation of her future success: "The glory of a firm, capacious mind." She easily passed the entrance exam for Sarah Lawrence, a progressive women's college with a reputation for an unstructured approach to higher education.

Opened in 1926 by educator Sarah Bates Lawrence, the college offered a liberal arts program in which students created their own curriculum, and traditional exams and grading were replaced by faculty reports. The school's proximity to Barbara's home offered her a measure of security, while her decision to live in a dormitory ensured that she would also feel independent. She spent the summer before her freshman year eagerly anticipating college life. But Barbara had only vague ideas about what she might study at Sarah Lawrence. Among other fields, she considered acting, writing, and teaching.

Most biographical sources report that Barbara graduated from college in 1953, but the date, like her birth date, is off by two years. As a member of the class of 1951, she attended college during years of significant national turmoil. America's "cold war" with the Soviet Union sparked a nationwide fear of Communism known as the "red scare." A process spearheaded by Senator Joseph McCarthy and a group of senators

organized as the House Un-American Activities Committee (HUAC) targeted government officials, artists, writers, and academics as suspected Communists or Communist sympathizers. Sarah Lawrence president Harold Taylor publicly objected to the committee's practice of forcing subjects of its investigations to sign oaths of loyalty to the U.S. government.

In the midst of this atmosphere of political protest and national fear, with students and faculty rallying regularly against the federal government's tactics, Barbara Walters remained apolitical. When she began dating Assistant U.S. Attorney Roy Cohn, a well-known compatriot of Joseph McCarthy, she seemed to her astonished friends to be unaware of the implications of such a visible association with "the other side." Most of her fellow students were not sympathetic, and a commentary in the class yearbook depicted Barbara as an ostrich with her head in the sand.

Politics did not hold Barbara's interest, but the theater did. The allure of performing before an audience drew her to take an acting class and, soon after, to audi-

Walters attended college in the midst of America's cold war with the U.S.S.R., yet classmates remember her as being surprisingly apolitical. For a short time, she dated Assistant U.S. Attorney Roy Cohn (left) without seeming concerned that he was an aide to Senator Joseph R. McCarthy of Wisconsin (right) during the senator's Communist "witch hunts."

tion for a school production of Sean O'Casey's *Juno and the Paycock*. Barbara landed the role of Mary Boyle, the daughter of an Irishman, but her East Coast accent and noticeable lisp were inappropriate for the play's setting. Her earnest efforts were unsuccessful, and she turned instead to writing about the theater.

As drama editor and movie critic for the school newspaper *The Campus*, Barbara revealed a talent for straightforward reporting and for insightful reviews of both school and off-Broadway productions. Her analytic abilities are evident in a review of August Strindberg's *The Father*: "'The Father' tells the story of a husband and wife who continually quarrel with each other in their efforts to gain supremacy in the home. However, in a larger sense, it is the story of 'the strife between the sexes,' man's conflict with woman, and their inability to really understand each other."

In addition to her strong professional ambitions, Barbara had other dreams. In her last years at Sarah Lawrence, she had a steady flow of suitors that kept the phones ringing at Titsworth dormitory. Other girls considered her a "social butterfly," but the outwardly self-assured Barbara privately worried whether the men she dated really liked her and whether one of the eligible young professionals would eventually be able to fulfill her ardent desire to marry and have children.

Socializing came second only to Barbara's studies during her college days. As a member of a small and close group of friends, she showed confidence and worked diligently to expand her popularity. She often used her parents' plush Manhattan apartment for small parties and for the group to meet their Friday night dates. In her junior year, her friends succeeded in getting her elected president of the dormitory, a position that showcased Barbara's maturity and her serious nature. Presiding over 40 dorm residents as an enforcer of school rules, she also acted as a "big sister" whom the girls sought out for guidance.

The summer after she graduated with a bachelor's degree in English, Barbara landed a series of part-time secretarial jobs before her father introduced her to Ted Cott, the vice president and general manager of WNBC, the New York City NBC television affiliate. By late winter she was writing press releases in the station's publicity, promotion, and advertising department—the first step toward a career that would elevate her to the pinnacle of television broadcasting.

College grad Barbara Walters was one of the handful of women to break into the "old boys' club" of broadcasting in the 1950s.

3

BREAKING
BARRIERS

In 1947, the year that Barbara Walters entered college, people received their news primarily through radio and newspapers. The news was reported largely by men; in the early history of broadcasting, before the invention of television, the handful of female voices that listeners heard on the radio were in programs targeting American housewives. The women covered topics of home and hearth, such as cooking, housekeeping, child rearing, education, sewing, and beauty tips; male radio personalities dominated the "hard news," such as sports, politics, crime, and war. Even the divisions of hard and soft news had been determined by male broadcasters.

The invention of television came upon the heels of advances in telephone and telegraph development. Scientists first added pictures to sound transmission at the beginning of the 20th century, but for decades they could only produce blurry images. By 1932, the technology had improved enough that NBC, a subsidiary of the Radio Corporation of America (RCA), began transmitting experimental telecasts from the Empire State Building in New York City. But television was still a new invention, and only the very wealthy invested in it. The station's short programs aired irregularly, roughly once a week for less than a half hour at a time.

In order for the television industry to grow, broadcasters and set manufacturers had to adhere to uniform standards. In 1936, the Federal Communications Commission (FCC) began holding hearings on the matter. Meanwhile, picture and sound transmission quality was becoming more refined, and by 1939, two other broadcasting companies—CBS and ABC—had emerged.

Beginning on July 1, 1941, the FCC authorized commercial television, and TV stations sprang up across the country. The world of journalism—and of entertainment—was changed forever.

Further developments in television were slowed by America's involvement in World War II, but when the war ended in September 1945, a frenzied production of black-and-white television sets began. The three networks, already in place, began broadcasting serials, variety shows, and news programs five nights each week.

By the time Barbara Walters graduated from college, 377 local stations were bringing television to nearly 90% of American homes, and most people had begun relying on the "tube" for their news. These broadcasts, like the radio programs of previous decades, were conducted primarily by men. In the early 1950s women broadcasters were rare; the television business was a classic example of an "old boys' club," a field in which male employers and employees predominated. The women who did make it on the air were rarely treated in the same way as their male counterparts; rather, they were expected simply to be pretty and charming and to dress like fashion models.

Despite such stereotypes and the sparse opportunities, several women did emerge as role models in the field of television broadcasting. Among them was Nancy Dickerson, who began in radio in 1954 and who

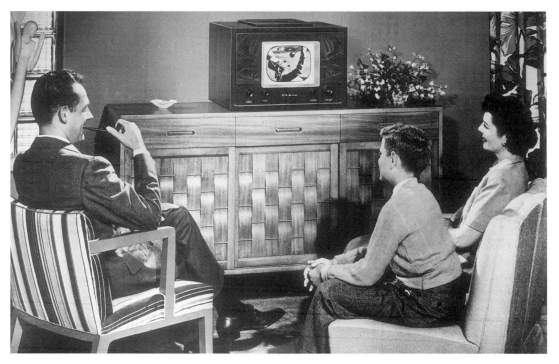

had become the most visible woman on television by the 1960s. In 1959, Dickerson convinced network executives to let her complete a report about army women who were stationed in Europe. Her work impressed Don Hewitt (later the executive producer of *60 Minutes*), who was then a producer of the *CBS Nightly News*, and he fought for her to be named the network's first female correspondent. (Ironically, in 1957 Barbara had consulted Hewitt for advice on her future. "You're a marvelous girl," he said, "but stay out of television.")

Meanwhile, Nancy Dickerson's counterpart at ABC, Lisa Howard, had landed her own afternoon newscast called *Lisa Howard and News with a Woman's Touch*. Marlene Sanders, a charter member of the National Organization for Women, was also on the roster of influential women in the early days of TV. On December 2, 1964, she became the first woman to anchor a network nightly news program when the regular

This 1948 television is a far cry from today's multimedia entertainment centers. By 1951, however, the "tube" had become a fixture in nearly 90 percent of American homes.

Actress Estelle Parsons, NBC's first Today *Girl, in 1952. When Barbara Walters landed the position 12 years later as the 34th* Today *Girl, it became more than just a cosmetic post; Walters was named a full-fledged* Today *reporter.*

anchor, Ron Cochran, fell ill. The record-setting broadcast received a double-edged review in the *New York Times*, which noted the significance of the event with a hint of condescension for the "courageous young woman with a Vassar [College] smile." Sanders later commented that the breakthrough had no effect on the male-dominated industry:

> It was as if it never happened. . . . People didn't begin to say, "Gee, what a great idea. Why don't we get a woman to anchor the evening news?" Of course, 1964 was the Dark Ages as far as women's progress was con-

cerned. Not only were women not an issue; no one was even thinking about them at all.

Women like Sanders had achieved high-profile positions and were earning more money than any of their predecessors, yet they were regularly reminded of their second-class status in the male world of broadcasting. Having entered the field during this era, Barbara Walters herself is considered a role model and barrier-breaker, though she insists that it was not her in particular but the social changes taking place in America that gave her an opportunity to break new ground:

> My contributions were relatively small. Because I was able to go off and interview a head of state and do a serious, good job, people could no longer say, "Only a man can do that, because the head of state won't take it seriously." But the success of women in TV and in other fields is because of the whole women's movement and the changes in this country. It's much more [women's rights activists] Gloria Steinem and Betty Friedan than it is Barbara Walters.

As late as 1983, however, Barbara remained the only woman to have served as a coanchor on a network nightly news program. Many women working in television today continue to name her as their professional role model, including high-powered talk-show host and entrepreneur Oprah Winfrey and broadcaster Paula Zahn.

Although Walters minimizes her role in laying the foundation for future women broadcasters, she rightly notes the changing political climate in the 1960s and 1970s that opened up opportunities for women in all fields. The Civil Rights Act of 1964 was originally intended to address racial prejudice. But a group of southern congressmen, eager to defeat the bill, added a provision outlawing gender discrimination. They believed that this addition would draw enough opponents to defeat the bill. Their plan backfired, however;

Barbara Walters on the set of the Today *show in the early 1960s. NBC hired Walters in 1961 as a temporary staff writer. She left the network 15 years later.*

the bill became law. As a result, a newly established federal agency known as the Equal Employment Opportunity Commission (EEOC), opened its doors in 1966. One third of the complaints that the new commission received were filed by women who claimed they were victims of workplace discrimination in terms of monetary compensation, benefits, job responsibilities, and opportunities for promotion.

In the decade that followed, affirmative action and enforced quotas continued to reshuffle the gender and ethnic ratios of the employment world, and their impact was felt sharply in television journalism. In 1982, the Radio-Television News Directors Association released a study showing that 36 percent of anchors in the United States were women, compared to 11 percent a decade earlier. The higher number of women appearing in front of the cameras was deceptive, however. Another study, conducted in 1980 by *Ms.* magazine, found that this increase did not accurately reflect the number of top management positions occupied by or available to women.

In 1953, 11 years before the Civil Rights Act was passed, an uncommon opportunity landed in the lap of the young college grad Barbara Walters. She was named the producer of a live, 15-minute, daily children's show on WNBC called *Ask the Camera*—becoming the youngest producer ever hired by the station. The show provided a means for Barbara to prove her professionalism and gain valuable behind-the-scenes experience. Recalling the assignment in a 1975 magazine article, Walters described what made the job an important experience: "the greatest aid to me—and something that many [newscasters] lack—was learning to cut and edit film," she recalled. Unfortunately, in 1954, almost as unexpectedly as she had been granted the opportunity, the station canceled the show. Barbara found herself suddenly unemployed.

The following year, however, two major events changed Barbara's life: she married 34-year-old businessman Bob Katz after a brief engagement, and she landed a job on the CBS *Morning Show*.

The *Morning Show* had entered the battle for daybreak viewers in 1954. It was originally cohosted by the distinguished newsmen Walter Cronkite and Charles Collingwood and rounded out with a weather "girl," a sportscaster, and a pair of puppets that pantomimed popular songs. In an attempt to compete with ABC's well-established *Today* show, CBS shuffled through a series of formats and staff members, including extending the program to two hours with Jack Paar as host, then reducing it to one hour and adding Dick van Dyke, who was cohost when Barbara joined the show. Barbara's duties ranged from researching and booking guests to generating story ideas.

Walters had apparently inherited her father's eye for talent and his flair for burlesque entertainment. One day she brought in an amateur archery champion and erected a straw target in the shape of the United States. While van Dyke read the regional weather forecasts, the archer shot arrows into the respective regions displayed on the map. The stunt amused viewers, and soon guests who could fling knives and shoot pistols were appearing on the show as well.

Walters often drew upon her personal interests as well as her father's show business contacts to come up with original story ideas. One of her early coups was a result of her interest in fashion—she gained her first on-air exposure when she substituted for a runway model who had not shown up for the program's fashion segment.

Network executives considered such segments a draw for female viewers, and Walters herself gladly covered stories of interest to women. "I never minded doing the so-called female things—the fashion shows, cooking spots, whatever," she said in a 1990 interview with *Ladies Home Journal*. "But at the same time, it did bother me that I wasn't allowed to participate in a Washington [political] interview. . . . That's why I started going out and getting my own interviews."

With her ultimate goal always in mind, Walters exhibited a clear understanding of what she had to do to make a name for herself. At 26, she had already developed a good reputation in the field. *Morning Show* producer Charlie Andrews remembered her as "ambitious, determined. You could see it in her eyes," and features coordinator Madeline Amgott observed, "She always knew she wanted to be in front of the camera."

In 1956 the network transformed the *Morning Show* into a new program called *Good Morning* with Will Rogers Jr. as host. Working again as a talent booker and all-around idea person, Walters arose every morning at 4:00 to arrive on time at the studio. In the young world

of television everyone was a neophyte, and Walters had gained a foothold at the right time, making connections with producers and directors that would serve her well in later years. As an integral part of the developing medium, she was also involved in many television firsts, including the first satellite telecast in 1965 and the first color broadcast of the *Today* show later in the same year.

Barbara did not rely solely on building working relationships, however. She worked diligently, racking up an impressive list of accomplishments. One early assignment in particular illuminates her talent for zeroing in on newsworthy subjects. On July 26, 1956, after a deadly collision between two ocean liners, the *Stockholm* and the *Andrea Doria*, she "scooped" the tales of some of the surviving passengers. Her producers praised her as a go-getter and entrusted her with an

Dave Garroway, the original host of the Today *show, during its first broadcast on Monday, January 14, 1952. The program is still on the air today.*

increasing range of critical assignments.

But these years were also difficult ones for Barbara, both professionally and personally. Audiences did not warm to Will Rogers Jr. on the *Morning Show*, which was now also competing with ABC's *Good Morning, America*. In 1957 the network canceled the show, and Barbara, once again unemployed, was forced to turn her attention to her deteriorating marriage. Her extremely long work hours had left little time for her to spend with her husband. Finally, in May 1958—only a few days before the grand opening of Lou Walters's last nightclub, the Café de Paris—a judge finalized Barbara's divorce from Bob Katz.

Lou Walters had sold his thriving New York Latin Quarter to finance the opening of his new cabaret. A month after its opening, the Café closed and Lou was bankrupt. Gone was his lavish Fifth Avenue penthouse with its splendid library and collection of fine art. He became embroiled in a tax evasion scandal shortly after. "Suddenly, I *had* to work," Barbara recalled in a 1982 interview:

> When my father went bankrupt, the same year that my marriage was finished, I had no choice any more. . . . I not only had to support myself but my parents and my sister. The government took away our beautiful home in Florida—everything.

It was then that Walters realized that she alone was responsible for her own financial welfare. "I knew I'd have to work all my life so I'd never feel financial pressure," she said.

Despite her concentrated efforts, Barbara failed to land another job in television. Deeply disappointed, she eventually took a $60-a-week position pitching clients as guests to radio and television producers at the public relations firm of Tex McCrary, Inc., in New York City. For the next two years, she worked under the supervision of William Safire, who would later become a speechwriter for President Richard Nixon, a *New York Times* columnist, and a bestselling author. For about five years, she worked to help her father recoup his losses. She later recalled these years as one of the low points of her life.

But what her new job lacked in salary, it made up in experience and in valuable industry contacts. Writing client profiles and press releases for local television and radio producers proved to be excellent training for an up-and-coming journalist whose living would one day depend upon landing interviews that held timely news and entertainment value. In fact, when Walters went to the *Today* show looking for a job, her association with Tex McCrary helped convince producer Fred Freed to give her a trial shot as a staff writer for 13 weeks.

The brainchild of broadcast pioneer Sylvester "Pat" Weaver (father of actress Sigourney Weaver), the *Today* show aimed for a unique format, blending news and entertainment. The show debuted on January 14, 1952, at 7:00 A.M., hosted by offbeat announcer Dave Garroway and his hairy sidekick, a chimpanzee named J. Fred Muggs. By the time CBS countered with its *Morning Show*, the *Today* show had become synonymous with America's morning routine, as indispensable as a first cup of coffee. In addition to Garroway, a host of well-known TV broadcasters attribute their success to early stints on the still vibrant *Today* show, including Hugh Downs, John Chancellor, Frank Blair, Frank McGee, Tom Brokaw, Jane Pauley, Bryant Gumbel, and Barbara Walters herself, who joined the show in 1961.

During her first year on the *Today* show, Walters's talent and hard work were evident in her shrewd decisions. For example, in the age before color television, she covered fashion week in New York City strategically attired in an all-white outfit, so that she practically glowed in the midst of the crowd surrounding her. Halfway through the season, the network brought in a new producer-host team, Shad Northshield and John

"I regretted that for years!" Barbara Walters has claimed about the day in 1962 when she opted to stay in her hotel room while on a press tour of India with First Lady Jackie Kennedy. Here's what Barbara Walters missed: Mrs. Kennedy and her sister, Lee Radziwill, ride a gaily decorated elephant through Jaipur, India.

Chancellor, and made Barbara a full-time writer. The aplomb with which she delivered an on-air summary for her first overseas assignment, a report on the Paris fashion season, ultimately helped her to land other choice assignments.

Until that time, Walters had been mainly restricted to writing the copy for five-minute segments sponsored by the S & H Green Stamp Company. The segments were read on the air by company spokesperson and former model Anita Colby. After Walters's successful on-screen debut, Northshield not only agreed to send her to cover the Paris fashion show the following year, but he also handed her the assignment that would become one of her early landmark stories: she became a member of the press corps that traveled with first lady Jacqueline ("Jackie") Kennedy on her 1962 goodwill trip to India and Pakistan. Despite her inexperience with covering a story of this magnitude, Walters jumped at the opportunity, determined to follow the lead of more seasoned reporters in the corps.

Mrs. Kennedy had been invited to India by Prime Minister Jawaharlal Nehru for a month-long excursion throughout the country. Although this assignment marked Walters's entry into the realm of hard news, she instinctively covered the human interest aspect of Mrs. Kennedy's appearances, from her hospital visit in New Delhi to a tour of the Taj Mahal palace to whimsical rides on elephants. Most of the first lady's comments were being filtered through her own press entourage, and Barbara, like many of the reporters on hand, felt some frustration at being held at arm's length from her subject. Unflappable—and resourceful—in the face of this challenge, Walters prevailed upon Letitia "Tish" Baldrige, Mrs. Kennedy's social secretary, to arrange for Walters to conduct a brief one-on-one talk with Mrs. Kennedy. Their private chat was a personal victory for the young reporter.

On the last day of the trip, an exhausted Barbara Walters decided to stay in her hotel room. That day, as she told an interviewer in 1996, "Jackie . . . called the female reporters together and gave each of them a little painted Indian box. I regretted [missing] that for *years*! . . . I saw her on all kinds of other occasions, but it was never quite the same."

When she returned home, Walters mined her experience for a wide range of professional exposure. She wrote a story for *Good Housekeeping* magazine about Lee Radziwill, Jackie Kennedy's sister, and featured Joan Braden, who had written the only authorized exclusive story about the trip, on the *Today* show. Despite her minor case of bad timing, Walters's intelligent and assertive reporting of Jackie Kennedy's trip boosted her reputation as a reporter. The formerly quiet schoolgirl was well on her way to becoming one of the best-paid journalists in American broadcasting history.

A woman on her way up: Barbara Walters in the 1960s. This photograph would later grace the cover of Walters's only book, How to Talk with Practically Anybody about Practically Anything, *published in 1970.*

4

THE MILLION-DOLLAR WOMAN

In 1962 Hugh Downs replaced John Chancellor as host in a major restructuring of the *Today* show. The change would have a profound effect on the pace of Barbara Walters's career. Downs became her ally and supporter. His admiration for her work helped convince producer Al Morgan to use her on many occasions in place of the "*Today* Girl," actress Pat Fontaine. Walters credits Downs with having given her the opportunity to appear regularly on the show and, consequently, with having raised her status in the field.

Since the show's inception, actresses, singers, or models, chosen for their glamour or maturity, had held *Today* Girl positions. As "decorative" additions to the staff, they read weather reports, covered light stories, and chatted with the host and his guests. Barbara got her big break on the *Today* show on November 22, 1963, when Morgan chose her to stand in for Fontaine. That day, President John F. Kennedy was assassinated by Lee Harvey Oswald. The shocked world seemed to have come to a standstill, and Walters was assigned to cover the aftermath of the tragedy. During her live, round-the-clock coverage, she showed extraordinary professionalism and a respectful measure of emotion and sensitivity. At one point during the telecast, she stayed on the air continuously for five hours, an accomplishment that Morgan considered her true coming-of-age in television.

In Barbara's personal life, meanwhile, her relationship with Lee Gruber, a producer and theater owner nine years her senior, was headed toward marriage. The couple had met in 1961 through mutual friends and had dated for two years. In December 1963, Barbara married Gruber in the company of a few close friends and family members. After settling into her second marriage, Walters once again set her sights on getting a permanent on-air position.

Walters learned that the *Today* show planned to let Pat Fontaine go, so she lobbied for the position of *Today* Girl. The network, which expressed reservations about her Boston accent and noticeable lisp, instead offered the job to Broadway actress Maureen O'Sullivan. But O'Sullivan had little live television experience and was unprepared for the position; she could not deliver quality interviews and reports. In addition, O'Sullivan and Hugh Downs fell into a pattern of polite but constant feuding. O'Sullivan was dismissed a few months later. Although Walters wished O'Sullivan no ill will, the woman's departure once again presented her with an excellent opportunity to land an on-air position. Downs himself fought to have Walters as his female counterpart, and some reports suggest that he refused to accept anyone else as a replacement.

In the end, Walters won the cherished position in October 1964 and set about tailoring the *Today* Girl persona to her own tastes. Aware of the burgeoning women's liberation movement, NBC took advantage of Walters's intelligence and creative flair and revamped the outdated *Today* Girl position, calling Walters the new *Today* reporter.

With the promotion came access to chauffeured cars

to the studio, a private office, a secretary, and a budget large enough to warrant the hiring of a business team to manage finances. Barbara also did something that no *Today* Girl had done: she hired a public relations firm to generate media coverage that quickly increased the public's interest in her.

The groundswell of publicity during Walters's first year in her new role transformed her from a reporter into a personality. A feature article in *Life* magazine praised her as the rising star of NBC with a headline that read, "Barbara Walters of 'Today' Show Looks Sharp—and Is Early to Rise, Wealthy and Wise." She was even invited by Johnny Carson to appear on the popular *Tonight* Show. Barbara herself was amazed at her growing celebrity status. She continued to work diligently, producing one impressive story after another. And viewers kept tuning in. Her success increased her self-confidence and inspired her to work even harder.

During her early years as a full-time reporter, Walters landed some of her most famous stories. In one instance, she even attended *Playboy* magazine president Hugh Heffner's "bunny school," a kind of training camp for young women who were hired to work in his nightclubs. She then waited tables in full bunny costume at one of his clubs, getting firsthand experience for her story on the other women who worked there. Other stories included an insider's account of the life of a policewoman and the marriage of President Lyndon B. Johnson's daughter Luci Baines to Ian Turpin.

With her skill in celebrity interviewing, Walters filled a void left when veteran broadcaster Edward R. Murrow's highly successful program *Person to Person* went off the air in 1961. She excelled at conducting the kind of intimate discussions with notable personalities that had made *Person to Person* popular. Her show-business background served her well. As the unofficial *Today* show celebrity interviewer, Walters landed interviews with entertainer Fred Astaire; diplomat Henry

Kissinger; and Mamie Eisenhower, the wife of former president Dwight D. Eisenhower, whom Barbara politely questioned regarding rumors of alcoholism. Mrs. Eisenhower revealed to Walters that she suffered instead from a disorder that affected her equilibrium and sometimes made her stagger and bump into things, appearing to be drunk.

Walters's *Today* stories were always impeccably researched and offered a unique blend of smart reporting and entertainment. Even when covering lesser-known events and people, she honed in on the public-interest aspect of her stories. For example, she reported on anti-Semitic housing practices in Michigan; the life of a Marymount nun; school dropouts; and a state reformatory for women in Wilmington, Delaware. She landed an impressive scoop with Dean Rusk, who had served as secretary of state for the Kennedy and Johnson administrations and resigned when Richard Nixon took office in 1969. Rusk granted her an exclusive interview and supplied enough hard news that *Today*'s producers aired a heavily promoted three-part series based on Walters's reporting. Himself a fan of Walters's, Rusk wrote her a letter in which he promised, "If any NBC vice-president gives you a hard time, show them this letter and tell them to leave you alone." The scoop drew envy from colleagues and confirmed Barbara Walters's reputation as a newsmaker in her own right.

In an era when women were still perceived as less serious reporters than their male counterparts, Walters proved that a woman could handle any assignment as well as a man could. Her daring and poise were especially evident in a memorable *Today* show segment shot in Wales, Great Britain, in 1971. Hugh Downs had retired from the show and had been replaced by Frank McGee. Walters, McGee, and Joe Garagiola, a former sportscaster who joined the show in 1967, were to enter a coal mine as part of the segment. After looking

into the mine shaft, McGee and Garagiola refused, but Walters, unruffled, entered the shaft and completed the assignment.

Some of Walters's colleagues have criticized her for her single-minded and even ruthless behavior when confronted with obstacles to her stories, her job, or her own publicity. The fact is that she is a perfectionist, insisting on the best lighting, the best scripting, and the highest level of professionalism from those who work with or around her. She is assertive in her demands, yet staffers from her tenure on the *Today* show also recall her warmth and friendliness. She made it a point to talk with staff members of all levels, from production assistants to writers, and her take-charge attitude often

Walters with her husband, Lee Gruber, and her adopted daughter, Jackie. "You have to want a child very badly if you're in this business," Barbara would say years later of her decision to raise a child while continuing to work full-time.

The newly published Walters prepares to autograph a copy of her book during a 1970 publicity tour.

came in handy when coworkers needed emotional or physical support. For example, Barbara once stayed awake all night with a distraught secretary who had just learned that she had a serious medical problem. In another instance, Walters secured the services of Vice President Spiro Agnew's doctor for a writer who had fallen ill while accompanying Walters on a trip to India. She then took on the woman's writing assignments in addition to her own and continued to nurse her coworker.

Walters's maternal instincts would soon have an outlet in her personal life. Having firmly established her career by age 39, she and her husband decided to adopt a child. She had had difficulty trying to carry her own child and had three miscarriages before making the decision to adopt. In June 1968, the couple brought home a baby girl, whom they named Jacqueline after Barbara's sister. Despite the demands of motherhood, however, Walters returned to her rigorous work schedule after only a few weeks of leave. Nearly as devoted to the *Today* show as she was to her daughter, she hired a cook and a nanny to help out at home. She loved being a mother and, like many new parents, carried baby pictures with her on assignments.

Almost 30 years later, Walters reminisced about what motherhood meant to her. "Jacqueline has been the home," she said in an interview with *McCall's* magazine in 1985. "[S]he is what makes it a home. I wanted a child *very, very* badly. You have to want a child very badly if you're in this business. I made the choice. I was not young; I already had a career." Barbara credits her daughter not only with creating a sense of home but also with providing a new perspective and the emotional insight that has enhanced her interviewing techniques.

As if her new child and her *Today* show responsibilities were not enough to keep her busy, Walters became one of 18 correspondents for producer Shad Northshield's 1969 three-hour special entitled "From Here to the Seventies." The retrospective on the previous decade was hosted by actor Paul Newman. Walters's contribution was a commentary on the "new sexuality" of the 1960s and opened with her frank discussion of birth control pills—a subject never before covered by prime-time television. Once again, Barbara Walters had made TV history.

By 1970, the star who could talk expertly, listen attentively, and charm regally wrote a book that attempted to capture the essence of her success. Walters's *How to Talk with Practically Anybody about*

Today *show coanchor Barbara Walters, newsmen Joe Garagiola (second from left) and Frank Blair (second from right), and coanchor Frank McGee in the early 1970s. Barbara briefly assumed a solo anchor position following McGee's death in 1974; Jim Hartz became her coanchor three months later.*

Practically Anything covered a range of social skills, including how to talk to celebrities, mingle at parties, and deal with difficult people, and it offered advice to the "average person" on how to cultivate important contacts. She also discussed the particulars of business and personal etiquette: how to write thank-you notes, send gifts, host dinner parties, and make follow-up phone calls.

But the overburdened newswoman had no time to flesh out and complete the book, so her publisher provided a ghostwriter named June Callwood, who expanded on the author's ideas and her initial outline. Barbara's fame, coupled with an expansive promotional tour, made the book a bestseller and a Literary Guild selection. During this period, Walters also contributed regularly to popular magazines like *Reader's Digest*, *Good Housekeeping*, *Ladies Home Journal*, and *Family Weekly*.

Meanwhile, she continued to be aggressive in pursuing insider news scoops for the *Today* show. President Richard Nixon, notoriously suspicious of the press, favored her as a reporter who could be trusted. Not only did Nixon give her privileged access to the White House and grant her exclusive interviews, but he also steered his foreign policy advisor, Henry Kissinger, to Walters for his first television interview, which he gave upon his return from an official trip to Hanoi during the later years of the Vietnam War. Kissinger and Walters have been friends ever since.

In 1972, Nixon also maneuvered Walters's interview with H. R. Haldeman, a powerful presidential consultant, and during the same week he named her one of three female journalists in the press corps covering his historic visit to China. Walters was criticized by some for giving in too easily to White House dictates, but the quality of her work was always high, and she earned a string of accolades.

Without question, Barbara Walters had become a successful and wealthy professional. But by 1970 she had already set her sights upon a new goal—landing a network news anchor position. To expand her news credentials, Barbara took over as moderator of a morning talk and public-affairs show on a local NBC affiliate station, WNBC-TV. The show, *For Women Only*, had earned high ratings and national syndication before Walters arrived.

In 1971, Walters replaced the regular host of the show, Aline Saarinen, who also reported on art and culture for the *Today* show and had been promoted to chief of NBC's Paris bureau. Walters renamed the show *Not for Women Only*, squeezing the show's taping schedule into her already frenetic work week, recording five half-hour shows in a single evening. In front of a live audience, she took on topical and often controversial issues, like marijuana use and the goals of the women's movement. She also generated creative formats for guest panels, such as the February 1972 five-part segment featuring the wives of the Nixon administration's cabinet members. The show's ratings tripled in Barbara's first six months as host; the *New York Times* dubbed *Not for Women Only* "one of the most improved and provocative shows in the entire early morning schedule."

In her new role, Walters proved that she could attract high-caliber guests, monitor discussions of political and social issues, and win NBC the ratings it needed to draw advertisers. Although she stayed with the show through 1975, she gradually reduced her involvement by alternating with former *Today* show host Hugh Downs.

In 1974, 52-year-old *Today* show cohost Frank McGee died of bone cancer. His death ended a tumultuous period in the show's history. McGee and Walters had never gotten along; during McGee's tenure, Walters was excluded from most Washington coverage and, by negotiated agreement, she could ask a guest a question only after her cohost had posed the first three. McGee made no secret of his dislike for Walters, and he sometimes took over her interviews in midstream. Her on-air personality appeared different as well: where Walters was the tougher of the Walters-Downs team, McGee's pit-bull personality often made her seem to be the "softer" of the new pair.

In her contract, Walters had demanded that she be automatically given the cohost slot should McGee ever leave the *Today* show. The network now had no choice but to give her the position—her reward for 12 years as a correspondent. On April 22, 1974, NBC announced her promotion, touting the show as "the only TV network news or public affairs program to have a female co-host." Three months after McGee's death, NBC

Walters receives a farewell hug from her former cohost Hugh Downs after her last appearance on NBC's Today *show in 1976.*

hired Jim Hartz to replace him. Hartz was the opposite of McGee in character and demeanor and got along well with Walters, who welcomed his sense of humor and pleasant personality.

Barbara Walters was famous. A 1974 *Newsweek* cover story proclaimed her "Star of the Morning." The *New York Times* regularly ran front-page coverage of her interviews. In 1975, she received the National Association of Television Program Executives Award of the Year; won her first Emmy for Outstanding Host in a Talk, Service, or Variety Series; and was named Broadcaster of the Year by the International Radio and Television Society. Shortly after, *Time* magazine named her one of the 100 most influential people in America.

But in the shimmering trail of her rising star, Barbara's personal life had once again deteriorated. She had separated from her husband, Lee Guber, in 1972; they divorced four years later.

Walters's next big project was a 90-minute special aimed at TV's afternoon soap-opera audience. The idea for the program, entitled "Barbara Walters Visits the Royal Lovers," began to brew after Barbara's *Today* show coverage of the royal families scored consistently high ratings. Among her most popular segments were the wedding of England's Princess Anne; coverage of the Duke and Duchess of Orléans, France, and of Queen Margrethe II of Denmark; and the investiture of England's Prince Charles. Aware of the public's fascination with the glamour and tradition of Europe's royalty, Walters convinced NBC to finance a special about them.

The show aired on September 25, 1975, preempting two of the network's most popular afternoon soap operas. But despite months of research and preparation and the show's elaborate settings, Walters's effort was panned as ridiculous and pretentious. The show may have been a critical disappointment, but its format provided an early blueprint for the *Barbara Walters Specials* that would make Walters a household name in years to come.

Around the same time, the *Today* show ran into difficulty. Its ratings had dropped sharply after Walters was paired with Hartz. Though the two got along well, Hartz appeared rather bland on the air. The sparks of the Walters-McGee partnership that had drawn viewers in the past were missing. But Walters was the linchpin of the show and she knew it. Nine months before her NBC contract expired, she began private contract negotiations with the network's executives. Her salary demands and her requests for perks, as well as her insistence on autonomy, made the executives balk, so Walters had her agent approach ABC. As it happened, ABC was looking for a new star.

In April 1976, Walters rocked the broadcasting industry with the announcement that she had signed a five-year, one-million-dollar-a-year contract to coanchor the ABC *Evening News* with Harry Reasoner. Although NBC made a counter-offer with a matching salary, they were unable to give her the position she had worked toward for years—a slot as evening news anchor.

In 1961, when Barbara Walters joined the *Today* show, she earned the Writer's Guild minimum pay of approximately $300 a week. No one would have guessed then that only 15 years later, she would become the first regular female coanchor on a network news program—and the highest-paid personality in television history.

Barbara Walters drew intense criticism when she became the broadcasting industry's first million-dollar anchorperson in 1976. Some believe that her detractors were reacting not against her qualifications, but against her gender.

5

A ROUGH ROAD

Barbara Walters's new position came with a salary that was in itself newsworthy—the highest ever paid to a network news anchor. When Barbara came on board at ABC, the network was languishing in last place in the competitive evening news ratings. Company executives hoped that she would be able to pull them out of this slump. The half-hour nightly news program was retooled to accommodate her reporting style, making room for interviews and extemporaneous dialogue as well as for a host of general interest feature stories on topics like health and personal finance. In addition, Walters's contract called for her to appear on a dozen episodes of the ABC current events show *Issues and Answers* and to host four specials each year. Because of these unique provisions, the news division of ABC paid only half of her salary; the other half was covered by the network's entertainment division. She also received a full-time secretary, a researcher, makeup and wardrobe consultants, a private office, and first-class accommodations while on assignment. No news personality, male or female, had ever earned such a huge salary or demanded such deluxe perks.

News of Walters's record-breaking deal drew criticism from both colleagues and the public. In a vitriolic piece on the change of personnel at ABC, *New Republic* magazine quoted veteran newsman Walter Cronkite, who lamented the decision by describing "the sickening sensation that we were all going under, that all of our efforts to hold television news aloof from show business had failed." The *New York Times* ran a story about the news with the headline "What Makes Barbara Walters Worth a Million?" Even Connie Chung, who was at the time a Washington correspondent for CBS, ridiculed ABC's decision, noting that Barbara was merely "an interviewer, a talk-show hostess; she does specials, not reporting, but *we* actually cover stories and then go back and report them."

The national outcry from the media in turn initiated a hotly debated public discourse on sexism in the workplace. Was the predominantly male field of broadcast journalism reacting against her qualifications or her gender? many people asked. Barbara's friend Hugh Downs has always believed that the problem was the latter. "I think a lot of insecure males were jarred by that contract, and they began to snipe at her," Downs said in a 1996 interview.

To make matters worse, a week after the announcement of her contract, the late-night comedy show *Saturday Night Live* presented the first skit to feature its now legendary "Baba Wawa" character. Created by comedian Gilda Radner, the character exaggerated Walters's real-life speech impediment—a difficulty that speech therapists call the "W-R substitution." Radner's comedic version of Walters became a regular and immensely popular character on *Saturday Night Live*, but it tagged Walters with an appellation that would follow her for the rest of her career. Walters has since come to terms with the ghost of "Baba Wawa," however. Almost 20 years later, *Saturday Night Live* again lampooned her in a skit called "The Bob Walders

Show," this time making light of her often-intimate interviewing style that has brought some of her subjects to tears. This time, she was able to laugh at the character, taking the jab as flattery rather than as an attack.

At the time, however, the fuss over her million-dollar contract profoundly distressed Barbara, and she felt even greater pressure to prove her worth. Perhaps the biggest problem threatening the success of her new venture—and her hopes for a smooth transition—was her relationship with her new partner, Harry Reasoner, who had been solo anchor of the *Evening News* for the previous year. Reasoner publicly disapproved of the network's decision to hire Walters, and he did not hide his distaste for her style of journalism. In his 1981 autobiography, *Before the Colors Fade*, Reasoner claimed that his difficulty was not with Walters personally. Rather, he had always believed that hiring her was a bad idea

Harry Reasoner made it clear that he strongly disapproved of ABC's decision to hire Walters as his cohost. While the two appear congenial following their first broadcast together, in time the hostility between them would become so strong that they would no longer be shown on camera together.

The late comedian Gilda Radner as "Baba Wawa," whom Radner patterned after Barbara Walters. The character delighted Saturday Night Live *viewers but Walters, under attack for her recently awarded $1-million contract, was not amused.*

because "whether it was a stunt or not, it was going to be perceived as a stunt." He also complained that the new format left too little time for reporting hard news. Statistically, this was probably true: the number of field reports from correspondents was reduced from 168 in the month before Walters joined the *Evening News* to 140 during her first month on the air.

Walters and Reasoner had never formally met before

Walters's contract was finalized; the closest they had come to working together was when both were members of the American press corps on Nixon's China trip. ABC attempted to smooth over the relationship between the two anchors by sending them out to lunch together before they began working with one another. ABC also boosted Reasoner's annual salary from $200,000 to $500,000—still only half of what Walters was earning. But the network's efforts to coach the pair in civility failed.

Barbara was not alone in the midst of this turmoil, however. Friends, colleagues, and even people she did not know personally flooded her with letters and notes of support—among them actor John Wayne, who sent her a telegram with the tough-guy command, "Don't let the bastards get you down." Barbara was charmed by the sentiment, especially since she and Wayne had never met (three years later, she conducted the last interview with Wayne before his death in 1979). TV fans also sent hundreds of letters of support and affection. Many of them came from women who related Walters's career battle to their own struggles. These well-wishers helped Walters to realize that not everyone wanted to condemn her. As always, she forged on.

One friend in particular helped her navigate the rough spots on this stretch of her career path—Alan Greenspan, who was then the chairman of the Council of Economic Advisors under President Gerald Ford. Walters had met Greenspan at a reception given by Vice President Nelson Rockefeller. The two became fast friends and frequent companions, fueling public conjecture about whether they were romantically involved. Barbara responded to the speculation by saying that Greenspan listened attentively during a time when she most needed a good friend.

After several weeks of rehearsal, the first broadcast of the *Evening News* with Barbara Walters aired on October 4, 1976. Walters was understandably nervous; she

Among those who offered support and encouragement to Walters during the stressful period following her move to ABC was her friend Alan Greenspan. The two are shown here in 1978 attending a film screening.

knew that she could not afford to make a major mistake. However, by the time she introduced one of the evening's biggest segments—her own taped satellite interview with Egyptian president Anwar Sadat—she had noticeably relaxed.

The media hype leading up to Walter's debut created a marked increase in the show's Nielsen score. Nielsen is a standard ratings system for television that measures a show's popularity in two ways: first, among all households that own televisions, and second, in "audience shares," or the percentage of households in which televisions are not only turned on but also tuned to the show. During the first days of the Walters-Reasoner pairing, the ABC *Evening News* Nielsen rating increased by a hefty 2.1 percent; by the end of two months, however, ABC came in last place behind CBS and NBC in evening news shows. The audience share for ABC had leveled off at its percentage during the week before Walters appeared.

Tension between Walters and Reasoner only increased with time. Within a few months, the two were no longer shown on camera together—a decision that reflected their distance off-camera as well. *New Republic* magazine articulated what had become obvious to the viewing public: "Harry Reasoner . . . seems as comfortable on camera with Walters as a governor under indictment." The coanchors' disdain for one another grew almost toxic. During coverage of Jimmy Carter's inauguration as president in January 1977, the two newscasters refused to sit near one another.

Before long, rumors began circulating that Walters was on her way out. Unflattering stories attacked her both professionally and personally. At one point, she even feared for her safety and that of her daughter, and she resorted to hiring bodyguards. In a 1997 interview with *Broadcasting & Cable* magazine, she described this year as "the worst period in my professional life."

This distressing point in her career was magnified by the death of her father on August 15, 1977. In spite of the ups and downs of life with Lou Walters, Barbara was deeply saddened by his passing and attributed some of her skills to his influence. In 1982 she described her father's charm:

> When he was in the money, my father gave us everything. He was sensitive, amusing, utterly cultivated, never without a book. If I have any writing ability, I get it from him. I loved him. All the people who worked for him *loved* him. But he was a gambler.

In the midst of these travails, Barbara Walters continued to work on other projects. She began to develop her first ABC special, which would include an

Barbara Walters prepares for a Today *show interview in 1976 with presidential contender Jimmy Carter while her daughter, Jackie, plays nearby. Later that year, Walters would draw flak for what some considered inappropriate questions during an interview with Carter and his wife, Rosalyn.*

intimate tour of her own Manhattan apartment, a sage strategy to show viewers and future guests that she was willing to put herself in the spotlight; an interview with singer Barbra Streisand; and an at-home chat with president-elect Jimmy Carter and his wife, Rosalyn. The show's production was rocky: Walters encountered several logistical problems and did not always agree with her producer.

The problems continued after the show aired on December 14, 1976. Many colleagues expressed dismay over what they considered inappropriate questions in the Carter segment. The first regarded a discussion of the Carters's sleeping arrangements. Walters asked whether the couple planned to take anything with them when they moved from their Georgia home to the White House. Would they, like first lady Betty Ford had, take along their bed? In reply, Carter asked whether Barbara wanted to know if he and Mrs. Carter slept in one bed or in separate beds. The exchange was taken out of context by members of the media and presented as though Walters had deliberately asked her subjects a very private question.

But it was her entreaty to Carter, who was then governor of Georgia, to "be wise with us, . . . be good to us" as president that caused the greatest outcry. A shocked Morley Safer lambasted Walters on his radio show, declaring that she had "effectively withdrawn herself from the profession of journalism" by straying from the objectivity required of a good reporter. Years later, reflecting on her final words to President Carter, Barbara explained her intention:

> That was the first special I did for ABC, at the height of the brouhaha over my salary. I wanted those specials to be different from news, to have a human quality. . . . At the end of the interview, [Carter] talked about what it meant to have been elected and what he hoped to do for the country; it was very moving. So I said, "Be wise, be kind." If I had to do it all over again, I probably would edit that out because it caused so much negative comment. But—well, what did I do that was so terrible?

Despite vocal criticism, Walters's program was a popular success, earning 36 percent of the audience share for its time slot. And because General Electric bought all of the allotted commercial time, the show produced a healthy profit for the network.

In 1977, Walters again made headlines as one of 14 American reporters to accompany Senator George McGovern to Cuba. The country's Communist leader, Fidel Castro, chose Walters to ride side-by-side with him in a Jeep through the Sierra Madre mountains as he steered with one hand and held his trademark cigar in the other. The interview made for extraordinary television images. Characteristically, Walters asked not only political and military questions but also more mundane, personal questions. Asking the leader whether he was married and whether he would ever shave off his signature beard, she would suddenly launch a straightfor-ward and hard-hitting question about Cuba's military presence in Angola. She spun the footage into an acclaimed hour-long special—another milestone to add to a growing list of world leaders who sought out Bar-bara Walters as a means to speak to the public.

Barbara has always considered herself a newswoman first, despite her success in interviewing celebrities and creating popular entertainment specials for ABC that attract corporate sponsors and earn substantial revenue. She believes that her image as a celebrity interviewer is partly a result of the network's concept of her role as a woman. A 1984 article in *Ladies Home Journal* described her attitude: "If she were a man, ABC would likely find a time slot in which she could do what she does best, that is, to bring people of significant social and political stature into America's living rooms." The network might encourage more hard news reporting from her, Barbara seemed to say, if she were male.

Nevertheless, Barbara Walters continued to create successful programs featuring Hollywood stars, such as her revealing interview with singer and actor Bing Crosby in 1977. During the program, Walters fired a string of questions at Crosby that targeted his religious and moral beliefs, specifically the touchy subject of pre-marital sex:

Walters: Suppose one of your sons came home and said, "Dad, I've got this girl and do you mind if we share a room here in the house?"

Crosby: In OUR house? No chance!

Walters: It happens in other families.

Crosby: Well, it wouldn't happen in MY family. If any one of them did that I wouldn't speak to them ever again.

Walters: Ever again?

Crosby: Ever again!

The dialogue had America glued to their TV sets; these were the very questions they themselves might like to ask but wouldn't dare, even if given the chance. Barbara pushed the limits of her guests' tolerance, but she did so with a gentleness and charm that elevated her interviews from rigid question-and-answer sessions to perceptive dramas. All the while, she remained calm and in control.

That same year, Walters conducted a momentous joint interview with Egyptian president Anwar Sadat and Israeli prime minister Menachem Begin. Sadat had made history by being the first Egyptian leader to make an official visit to Jerusalem; Walters made history by bringing the two together in dialogue. After insisting on equal access, CBS newsman Walter Cronkite and

Among Barbara Walters's groundbreaking accomplishments is her historic 1977 interview with Cuban leader Fidel Castro. Although she claimed in a 1990 interview that the dictator "talked too long," she also admired his "humor and sparkle."

NBC's John Chancellor were also granted joint interviews, although theirs were conducted after Barbara's.
As a result of the interviews, the three reporters were
awarded the $10,000 Hubert H. Humphrey Freedom
Prize by the B'nai B'rith Anti-Defamation League for
promoting peace in the Middle East.

In January 1978, ABC hired Roone Arledge to head
the news division of the network. His first mission was
to revive the quickly withering *Evening News*, which
was foundering under the unfortunate Reasoner-Wal-
ters pairing. To achieve this, Arledge initiated widespread changes. At first he tried to keep Reasoner and
Walters apart by giving Walters more assignments outside of the studio. But the new arrangement did not
work, and on June 1, Reasoner resigned, announcing
that he was returning to his former employer, CBS.
Happily, Reasoner and Walters eventually made
amends, and Walters even interviewed her former coanchor during the promotion of his autobiography.

After Reasoner's departure, Arledge unveiled a new
format for the ailing show, renaming it *World News
Tonight* and operating with three anchors stationed in
different cities: Peter Jennings in London, Max Robin-
son in Chicago, and Frank Reynolds in Washington,
D.C. (Jennings would become sole anchor of *World
News Tonight* in 1983). Meanwhile, Walters remained
in New York City at the "Special Coverage Desk,"
where she conducted big-name interviews. Though the
reorganization was a demotion of sorts for her—she no
longer announced or read the news—Walters claimed
that she had wanted this kind of position all along.
"From the day I was hired," she said, "I asked them not
to put me on the air *just* to read."

While Walters continued to land high-profile interviews, her own fame was rapidly growing. She was in
demand as a lecturer and as a contributor to several
magazines and newspapers. She even made cameo
appearances in two feature films, *Goin' South* (1978)

and *Rock 'n' Roll High School* (1979). But as she approached the renewal date of her ABC contract in 1981, Walters was determined to redefine her role at the network. After rejecting an offer from CBS to join their weekly news program *60 Minutes*, Walters signed a new five-year contract with ABC that provided her with three of her own specials each year, occasional hard news assignments, and regular appearances on *20/20*, a newsmagazine show hosted by Hugh Downs. That same year, she also began filling in for David Hartman on *Good Morning, America* and for Ted Koppel on *Nightline* when either host was out.

By this time *20/20*, once tagged "dizzyingly absurd" by the *New York Times*, had developed into a consistent top-25 ratings winner, paving the way for the other networks to launch similar newsmagazine shows like *Dateline NBC*. ABC had offered Walters a regular spot on *20/20* years earlier, but she had declined. At the time, she was just emerging from her difficult year as coanchor with Harry Reasoner and was recovering from the damaging furor over her salary. Now, however, Walters began to feel that the highly rated newsmagazine show would provide a comfortable home base for her. The program, which covers both breaking news and stories with wide-ranging human interest, would expose her to a larger mass audience than ever before and seemed to offer the right blend of news and entertainment. There was only one problem—Walters wanted to be a cohost rather than a contributor.

Although Downs has great respect and admiration for Walters, he ardently objected to sharing the anchor desk with her on *20/20*. He believed that coanchoring the program would be awkward because ABC had promised him sole hosting responsibilities and Barbara would be perceived as the "star" of the show. In the end, the two worked out a compromise: Downs would remain the solo host, while Walters would handle the ad-lib discussions with correspondents who contributed pieces. At the end of each program, Downs and Walters would appear together to wrap up the show. This division of labor continued until the fall of 1984, when ABC officially named Walters cohost. Today, each episode ends with her signing off by saying, "We're in touch so you'll be in touch," and with Downs giving the final goodnight.

Downs's and Walters's disagreements over their roles on *20/20* have not changed their warm regard for one another. Walters still speaks about Downs with fondness and attributes her success to his instrumental role in her early career. "If Hugh had not fought for my opportunity to appear regularly on *Today*, I would not have happened in this business," she told *Good Housekeeping* magazine in 1992. Downs, in contrast, gives her all the credit for her own success: "[I]n truth, she discovered herself," he said in the same interview. "With her talents, she would eventually have happened without me."

One of Barbara's most famous interviews—and one which she cites again and again as one of the most affecting of her career—was her 1981 talk with Academy Award–winning actress Katherine Hepburn, whose outlook on marriage, family, and career touched upon Barbara's own struggles to "have it all." At the time of the interview, Barbara herself was feeling insecure and indecisive about her own life choices and about her attempts to juggle motherhood and a demanding career. By contrast, Hepburn was emphatic and definitive about her own choice of a career over domesticity. She said that if she were a man, she would not marry a woman with a career, and that she herself had never wanted children because their needs would have been a source of resentment for her in her attempts at professional success. Walters found Hepburn "dogmatic, opinionated, brave, and smart," and their meeting influenced her profoundly.

Years later, Walters acknowledged that she had had

more freedom than most women to pursue both a family and a career. Even so, she had not chosen an easy way to conduct her life. But her influence on how TV presents news, information, and people is apparent in nearly every prime-time information program on the air today, including such viewer favorites as *Dateline NBC* and ABC's own *PrimeTime Live*.

Hugh Downs and Barbara Walters on the set of 20/20 in 1988.

6

STAR POWER

As a regular on *20/20*, Barbara Walters developed a type of interview that had rarely been seen on television. She saved the movie-star interviews for her *Barbara Walters Specials*. For this more serious program, she began to seek out everyday people who had been suddenly thrust into the public spotlight, especially people at the center of controversies or those accused of criminal activity. Some of her most acclaimed interviews include Jean Harris, who was convicted of murdering the "Scarsdale Diet" doctor Herman Tarnower; Claus von Bulow, a Danish socialist accused of poisoning his wife; Donna Rice, whose affair with Gary Hart cost him the Democratic presidential nomination; tennis star Arthur Ashe, after he had announced that he was HIV-positive; and the controversial assisted-suicide doctor Jack Kevorkian. When the Gulf War ended, Barbara was the first to interview General Norman Schwarzkopf, who had commanded U.S. forces during the conflict. Walters managed to record the general admitting that he believed the war had ended too soon.

With Barbara Walters sharing the helm, *20/20* became even more successful, as the public revealed a voracious appetite for firsthand

During a startling 20/20 interview with heavyweight boxer Mike Tyson and his wife, Robin Givens, in September 1988, Givens confirmed rumors that Tyson was physically abusing her. Walters interviewed Givens again the following month.

explanations, unrehearsed responses, and faces contorted with strong emotions. Walters leads viewers through the interview process guided by the conviction that "interviewing *is* reporting. . . . History is biography." She carefully advises each subject before and in between takes, dispensing practical and friendly suggestions on how best to conduct oneself during the interview.

A breakthrough came in 1987, when Barbara's talent for creating an impact led to a full-hour interview with heavyweight boxer Mike Tyson and actress Robin Givens, who was then his wife. The show aired in the wake of widespread reports that Tyson suffered from manic depression and had been physically abusing Givens. In a surprising turn of events, Givens herself spoke with forthright anger and honesty about Tyson's frequent violent outbursts, describing their marriage as "worse than anything I could possibly imagine." That episode of *20/20* earned extremely high ratings and established Barbara Walters as one of ABC's most visible and valuable stars.

But Walters was growing weary of the interview format for which she was well known. She had admitted some years earlier that she didn't care for the actual process of interviewing anymore. "[W]hat I hate is the preparation of the questions," she said in 1984. "People say, 'Oh, isn't it fun?' It *isn't* fun!" She especially dislikes conducting celebrity interviews—those for which she is perhaps most famous and that generate greater revenues and higher Nielsen ratings. Many celebrities, she explains, agree to interviews as a way to promote a new book, film, record, or television show. During a promotional tour—in a concentrated period of time—such celebrities will appear on nearly every morning show and, as Walters puts it, will "spend four minutes [interviewing] . . . plug their movie, and . . . walk off." The great challenge for Walters is to "get them to say something interesting" that no other interviewer has learned. In 1996, Walters stipulated in her contract renewal with ABC that she do fewer celebrity interviews.

On May 10, 1986, Barbara took a rare vacation from working to marry Merv Adelson, the chairman of Lorimar Productions, whom she'd met two years earlier on a blind date arranged by a mutual friend. As with her professional life, this part of Barbara's personal life also became a news item: she had been single for 14 years, and until her marriage to Adelson had dated several men occasionally. Gossip columnists had routinely pondered over which one she might marry.

Walters and Adelson were married in a private wedding ceremony at the home of friends in Beverly Hills, California. Barbara's daughter, Jacqueline, came in from an Idaho boarding school to serve as her mother's maid of honor. Typical of the couple's high-powered lifestyles, the newlyweds both returned to work two days later, Adelson in Los Angeles and Walters in New

York. This bicoastal arrangement worked well for the
first few years. Eventually, however, the strain of work
and distance led to a separation in 1990. They divorced
in 1992 after six years of marriage.

Regardless of the ups and downs of her personal life,
Walters continued her hectic career pace, producing as
many as 12 specials and investigative reports annually
for *20/20*. These included coverage of such important
social issues as adoption, AIDS, working mothers, and
education. In December 1986, though, one such
report resulted in personal scandal, not for her subject
but for Walters herself.

Walters interviewed two men who played pivotal
roles in the Iran-Contra arms deal: Saudi Arabian businessman Adnan Khashoggi and Iranian arms dealer
Manucher Ghorbanifar. After the interview, Ghorbanifar asked Walters to deliver to President Ronald Reagan
confidential documents that reportedly contained information about payments made to Iranian officials. She
reluctantly agreed, believing that the information might
help expedite the release of American hostages held in
Iran and that her actions might help to save lives.

Shortly after the interview, the *Wall Street Journal*
broke the story on Walters's "involvement." Because
she had seemingly acted as a private go-between for a
government agency and because she had withheld the
content of the messages from the public, she was
strongly and widely criticized by both the public and the
media. In an official statement, ABC admitted that Walters had "violated a literal interpretation of news policy."
The network ultimately stood by its reporter, dismissing
the idea of imposing formal disciplinary action and
asserting that she had given all of the information she
received to ABC. The network's editors, however, could
not verify the validity of the information.

In the same year, Walters's huge ratings and growing
celebrity status landed her a third five-year contract with
ABC—this time, with an annual salary of nearly three

million dollars, roughly matching that of veteran *Nightline* anchor Dan Rather. No other female newscaster had been on the air as consistently and for as many years as Barbara Walters. Along with a handful of well-respected female reporters like Lesley Stahl, Kathleen Sullivan, and Lynn Sherr, Walters led the way for the next generation of powerhouse newswomen, including Diane Sawyer, Connie Chung, Jane Pauley, and Katie Couric.

In interviews on the subject, Barbara routinely expresses pride in her female colleagues and in their growing list of accomplishments. She has always maintained that the image of her as an early role model for aspiring newswomen should be viewed from the perspective of the other women who also broke new ground in broadcasting.

Although opportunities for women in television news, at least in front of the camera, have grown since television's debut, the field still remains largely a "man's world" in some respects. As late as 1994, media critic Jon Katz spoke of the stubborn double standard that continues to affect women in the industry, a situation that he called the "glamour-girl" lock on TV news, meaning that women are still sometimes chosen for their looks rather than their expertise or talent. "It's like what MGM [movie studio] did with [actress] Jean Harlow—making stars out of the glamorous women rather than letting them do serious journalism," Katz remarked. "But that's the way you create a journalistic superstar now—build big mythologies about them and their careers, and promote them heavily. . . . Barbara is . . . the queen, by dint of her age and seniority and star power."

Barbara Walters and Merv Adelson pose for photographers moments after their wedding on May 11, 1986.

Male journalists have never been subjected to the same public scrutiny of their personal lives; nor do they attract the same avid interest in their ages and physical attributes as do their female counterparts. In some instances, this double standard is not only unfair but also illegal. In 1983, for example, Kansas City anchorwoman Christine Craft sued KMBC-TV, where she worked, for having demoted her from an on-air position because of her appearance. Craft claimed that the station had removed her from the air because she was beginning to look "old and unattractive." She won the case and was awarded $500,000 in damages.

Many observers regarded the outcome of this case as a major victory in the battle for gender equality in the workplace. Others believe that youth and beauty will continue to influence network decision-makers who operate under constant pressure to win big ratings and that discrimination has not abated. Seven years after Craft's milestone lawsuit, NBC created a stir when it announced the replacement of *Today* show host Jane Pauley with Debra Norville. Pauley had recently become a mother, and Norville, touted for being younger and "blonder," was scheduled to take her place. In this atmosphere, Barbara Walters's staying power and consistent appeal are even more remarkable.

Many of the women in newscasting themselves acknowledge how tough it is to achieve success in their field. Despite the competition, they regularly credit one another with helping to improve opportunities for women in broadcasting and often praise the accomplishments of their female colleagues. "We all have an investment in each other's future," Paula Zahn maintains. "The more each of us succeeds, the better off we all are. We'll still be competitors, but we'll be better competitors."

Unfortunately, another aspect of the industry's double standard is that rivalries among women are often trumped up by other media into "cat fights." In 1994

Kansas City anchorwoman Christine Craft leaves a federal courthouse in Joplin, Missouri, in 1984. Craft's successful lawsuit against her former employer highlighted the persistent double standard operating in the broadcasting industry.

Barbara found herself portrayed as a media queen competing against ABC colleague Diane Sawyer, coanchor of *PrimeTime Live*, a popular news and investigative program.

PrimeTime Live and *20/20* are the two most-watched weeknight newsmagazines on television. Perhaps for this reason, the shows' anchors were viewed as "rival mega-stars" by the *Washington Post*—dueling for the favor of their fans and for their survival at the network. Some reports even claimed that Walters had attempted to convince Sawyer's slated guests, including Katherine Hepburn and the parents of John Hinckley Jr. (the man convicted of attempting to assassinate President Ronald Reagan), to appear with her on *20/20* instead.

Both Walters and Sawyer maintained that their competition is friendly. "I think ABC will tell you this," Walters said in a 1994 interview with *Vanity Fair* magazine:

> Peter Jennings and Ted Koppel [both of ABC] are far more competitive in their stories, in what they have to do, than the women. . . . It's part of this whole cliché

about women. I mean, if you hear that Ted and Peter are arguing about which one of them should go to Rwanda, you'd never talk about the catfighting. It would be these two great gentleman.

Diane Sawyer, whom *Vanity Fair* interviewed jointly with Walters, agreed, adding that male news anchors are perhaps even less willing to share the spotlight than their female counterparts are. "I can't imagine [that] the same level of disclosure and intimacy and collegiality took place before women got into the business," Sawyer remarked.

Undeniably, both ABC shows often compete for the same guests. But Walters and Sawyer discredit the idea that either has cause to covet the other's stories or begrudge the other's accomplishments. Their exclusives in 1994 alone demonstrate a healthy competition—and two distinct talents for landing impressive interviews: while Sawyer featured the jailed and denounced Panamanian president Manuel Noriega; figure skater Tonya Harding, who was accused of planning an assault on her competitor Nancy Kerrigan; and Russian president Boris Yeltsin, Walters captured Wall Street trader Michael Milken's first televised confession of wrongdoing; Black Muslim leader Louis Farrakhan in a rare interview; and Senator Bob Packwood, who had been accused of sexual harassment.

One of Barbara Walters's most famous and most successful interviews aired on September 29, 1995. On that evening, 29 million Americans tuned in to watch her speak with actor Christopher Reeve, who had been paralyzed four months earlier in a riding accident and is now confined to a wheelchair. Although scores of journalists had tried to secure a first post-accident interview with Reeve and his wife, Dana, Barbara Walters alone was granted the opportunity.

As often happened, the story of her landing the interview became a news item in itself. The Reeves said that they wanted to make a public appearance to raise

awareness of spinal cord injuries and to raise money for research and treatment in the field. But it was also important to them that their story was not trivialized or sensationalized. "[A]fter watching Barbara Walters for so many years [I felt] that she would be the best qualified to help us with that," Christopher Reeve said later.

With extraordinary compassion, Walters gave her viewers a moving and insightful look at the Reeves and at their tragedy and strength in its aftermath. She was able to make the couple feel comfortable while they spoke about the most intimate details of their lives. Christopher Reeve recalled:

> She made us feel unselfconscious. And that allowed the television audience to see two people as they really are. . . . Barbara gave us room to express [the despair I once felt] and also to talk about how much joy, hopefulness, laughter and love remain in our life.

ABC colleagues Diane Sawyer (left) and Barbara Walters with publisher Katharine Graham during a 1991 "Women's Power Lunch." Despite persistent rumors to the contrary, Sawyer and Walters claim that their professional rivalry is friendly.

Walters meets for the first time with the family of murder victim Ron Goldman for the September 16, 1994, edition of 20/20.

The interview deeply affected Barbara. She recalls in particular one moment when Dana Reeve described how Christopher felt when he first regained consciousness after the accident. He suggested to his wife that he "check out," or end his life. In response, Dana had touched his head and said, "*This* is who you are, not your body." For Walters, the story highlighted the importance of looking beyond physical appearances for the real essence of a human being. She was struck not only by the Reeves' courage and lack of self-pity but also by "the message that you are your mind, you are your intelligence."

For this reason, she feels that the Reeve interview was the one that most affected her personally. "I think this interview had a greater effect than anything that I have done in all the years at ABC, because there are not that many times when you come across that extraordinary true, shining love that Chris and his wife have for each other."

On May 6, 1996, a few days after Walters's 20th anniversary broadcast, she received the prestigious George Foster Peabody Award for her interview with Christopher and Dana Reeve. Even more important, after reviewing a videotape of the award-winning interview, the United States Senate increased the national budget for spinal-cord injury research in America.

Walters believes that her ability to identify emotionally with people in difficult predicaments comes from having grown up with a mentally disabled sister. "I think I have a real empathy for those who have to overcome tremendous obstacles," she said in 1995. "My favorite interviews are not with heads of state or celebrities, but with people like [paralyzed policeman] Steven McDonald or the pitcher [and cancer survivor] Dave Dravecky."

The drama of another very public—and this time very controversial—tragedy was also revealed to TV viewers by Barbara Walters. In September 1994, three months after Nicole Brown Simpson and her friend Ronald Goldman were murdered, Goldman's family granted their first interview to Walters. The Goldmans openly expressed their grief and their anger toward football legend O. J. Simpson, Nicole Brown's estranged husband, who was later accused and acquitted of the murders during a criminal trial.

On four more occasions, as the trial wore on, Walters tracked the Goldmans' emotional fight to achieve justice on behalf of their son and brother. Their final exclusive interview with Walters ran after the 1997 publication of the family's book, *His Name Is Ron*, and shortly after a civil jury, in a second trial, announced Simpson's guilt. In the Goldmans' symbolic hour of vindication, Barbara questioned them as a trusted confidante might. She asked about Ron Goldman's biological mother, who had received a portion of the civil jury's multimillion-dollar award. They discussed how the family felt about the money that the Brown family received for the support of the two Simpson children. They made no secret of their dislike of the prosecutors in the criminal trial, and then, near the end of the segment, the Goldmans allowed themselves to think about the future.

The Goldmans were not the only figures related to the Simpson murder trials who chose to confide in Barbara Walters. She also interviewed Cora Fishman and Kris Jenner, two of Nicole Simpson's friends. Brian "Kato" Kaelin, an employee of Simpson's who became an unwitting celebrity after testifying during the criminal trial, also appeared several times on *20/20*. Defense attorneys Robert Shapiro and Robert Kardashian eventually discussed their roles with Walters as well.

Among all the interviews Barbara Walters conducted with those associated with the murder and subsequent trials, one of the most riveting was with Marcia Clark, the lead prosecutor from the Los Angeles District Attorney's Office, who fought what would become her final court case under the watchful eye of the public. With the trial being broadcast live every day, Clark, the other attorneys involved, and Judge Lance Ito became public figures, forced into the limelight as if they themselves were the celebrities or criminals. Clark had been harshly criticized for her litigation style, and her tumultuous personal life was thrust into public view.

In a two-part interview in May 1997, Barbara posed difficult, intriguing questions about the private and professional aspects of Clark's life. She opened her profile by asking about the speculations over Clark's relationship with her colleague Christopher Darden, and she moved gently onto another sensitive subject, the question of gender bias in the courtroom. Walters's interview displayed her potent mix of compassion and knowledge and her talent for asking hard-edged, probing questions that might sound like cross-examinations in another interviewer's hands. Reminding Clark of the times when the lawyer's hairstyle changes made the nightly news, Walters asked, "How did that make you feel?" And when she referred to rumors that Clark had checked into a rehabilitation clinic after the trial, Walters was strikingly direct. "Let's—well, let's put them to rest," she said to Clark. "Did you?"

But sharing juicy tidbits with viewers is not Barbara Walters's sole purpose in interviewing celebrities and other personalities. She has also been praised for being fair and open-minded—so much so that her detractors have accused her of being overly liberal. Others commend her commitment to covering groundbreaking issues not usually discussed on prime-time TV, as she did during her interview with HIV-positive Olympic gold medalist Greg Louganis, who spoke with Barbara after revealing that he is gay. As a result of this interview, on March 17, 1996, Walters received the first Excellence in Media Award from the Gay and Lesbian Alliance Against Defamation (GLAAD), which honored Walters's fair, accurate, and inclusive representation of gay and lesbian issues.

The Clark and Louganis interviews again showed the style that viewers had come to expect from Barbara Walters. She has developed an on-air image both as the girlfriend to whom one turns in time of need and as an authority figure who has earned the right to demand the truth.

The cohosts of the unique daytime talk show The View, *from left to right: Star Jones, Joy Behar, Meredith Vieira, Debbie Matenopoulos, and Barbara Walters, whose Barwall Productions coproduces the program.*

7

RETURN TO DAYTIME

"I was very happy," Barbara Walters said in 1987 of her stint on the *Today* show. "But I would never go back and do another morning show." Ten years later, she proved herself wrong by becoming one of the hosts of a uniquely formatted daytime talk show called *The View*.

With her roots in daytime television, Barbara responded to ABC's request for new program ideas with *The View*. In a deviation from the traditional taped daytime talk shows, the new hour-long show, created by Walters and Bill Geddie, the executive producer of her specials, is broadcast live from New York City five mornings a week at 11 A.M. Besides Walters, the show features four smart and accomplished women of different ages and backgrounds: Meredith Vieira, a former CBS news correspondent and veteran (like Walters herself) of ABC's *Turning Point*, who acts as the leader of the group; ex-prosecutor and television legal reporter Star Jones; 23-year old former MTV staffer Debbie Matenopoulos; and comedian

Pop musician Elton John was among those featured in the 1997 edition of Barbara Walters's popular annual special highlighting the year's "10 Most Fascinating People."

Joy Behar, who appears three days each week when Walters is off. Barbara has a special role in seeing *The View* take shape. Unlike her other responsibilities with ABC, she is the executive producer of the show, and her Barwall Productions company shares the program with the daytime division of ABC.

Aiming for a cordial and comfortable atmosphere, as though they were friends speaking their minds, the cohosts of *The View* shift from intelligent conversation to lighthearted banter. They also interview a variety of guests, including celebrities, renowned experts, and self-help authors. They encourage audience participation as well. A sampling of the show schedule from its second week on the air reveals a wide range of current topics and entertaining guests, including former White House press secretary George Stephanopoulos; Broadway and television star David Alan Grier; actress Isabella Rossellini; and a representative from the anti-pornography group "Enough is Enough," discussing the group's efforts to protect children from pornography on the Internet.

At the close of each show, the four women and their guests answer a question of the day. These range from the frivolous to the serious. On ABC's Internet site, TV viewers have a chance to answer the question of the day themselves, review the survey results, and suggest future questions.

The premiere week of *The View* received mixed reviews. Among those who praised the program was *People* magazine, which complimented the format and the experience of its hosts (except Matenopoulos, who was noted for her inexperience). The *New York Times* also lauded the show for its "renegade spirit" and Barbara Walters for her guiding vision. Complimenting the woman who, for more than 30 years, has contributed to the breakdown of gender barriers in television and to the dismantling of preconceived ideas about so-called women's stories, the *Times* reported:

> [Walters] and her production company deserve full credit for guiding this show in such a smart direction. During hot topics, it is often her voice that marks out some complicated middle ground and prevents 'The View' from becoming 'Crossfire for Girls.' This show

dares to assume that women, even those watching at home in the morning, have minds of their own.

These days, Barbara Walters spends the little free time she has with her current companion, Virginia senator John W. Warner. She maintains a close relationship with her daughter, who now lives in the Pacific Northwest. Walters makes her home in New York City and is often spotted lunching at her favorite Manhattan bistro there, Cafe des Artistes.

Walters has received a number of honorary degrees, from Ohio State University, Temple University, Marymount College, Wheaton College, and Hofstra University, among others. The television industry continues to shower her with awards as well. Recently, the National Association of Broadcasters (NAB) selected her as recipient of the 1997 Distinguished Service Award for her significant and lasting contribution to the American system of broadcasting. Presenting the award, NAB president Edward O. Fritts called her "one of the world's most respected interviewers and journalists. . . . she is one of America's great news personalities."

Throughout the evolution of television, Barbara has not only worked at the top of her game but has also become something of an icon in broadcasting. It seems at times that she is everywhere: in addition to her producing and hosting duties for *The View*, her coanchor position on *Turning Point*, and her work on her many *Barbara Walters Special*s, she now makes a second weeknight appearance on *20/20*, following the network's addition of a Monday night show in 1997. Clearly, Barbara Walters has no intention of slowing down.

In 1996, Walters's colleague and friend Mike Wallace of CBS's *60 Minutes* summed up Barbara's standing in the world of television: "Don't you dare say 'successor' to Barbara. . . . She is an institution now.

She has become the celebrity saint." Walters may have imitators and admirers—and many qualified and talented women may be ready to take her place—but no one can reproduce her indomitable style or her remarkable professional record. There is only one Barbara Walters.

CHRONOLOGY

1929	Born on September 25 in Boston, Massachusetts
1947	Graduates Birch Wathen High School, New York City
1951	Receives a B.A. in English from Sarah Lawrence College, New York
1952	Works in the promotion department at WNBC-TV; becomes the station's youngest producer the following year
1955	Marries Bob Katz; hired as a staff writer for the CBS *Morning Show*
1958	Divorces Bob Katz
1961	Joins NBC's *Today* show as staff writer
1963	Marries Lee Guber
1968	Adopts daughter, Jacqueline
1970	Publishes her book, *How to Talk with Practically Anybody about Practically Anything*
1971	Hired as host for *Not for Women Only* by WNBC-TV in New York
1974	Becomes first female coanchor of the *Today* show
1975	Wins her first Emmy Award for work on the *Today* show
1976	Begins one-year stint coanchoring the ABC *Evening News* with Harry Reasoner; divorces Lee Guber
1977	Father, Lou Walters, dies on August 15
1978	Awarded the Hubert H. Humphrey Freedom prize from the Anti-Defamation League of B'nai B'rith
1979	Becomes a regular contributor to *20/20*
1980	Wins Emmy Awards for Best News Program Segment and Best News, shares a third Emmy for Best News and Documentary Program for her work on *Nightline*
1983	Wins Best Interviewer Emmy Award
1984	Named cohost (with Hugh Downs) of *20/20*
1985	Wins two Emmy Awards for her *Barbara Walters Specials*; sister, Jacqueline Walters, dies in November
1986	Marries Merv Adelson
1988	Mother, Dena Walters, dies in June
1990	Becomes the first woman inducted into the Academy of Television Arts and Sciences' Hall of Fame
1992	Wins Emmy Award for a *Barbara Walters Special*; divorces Merv Adelson
1994	Named coanchor of ABC's *Turning Point*
1997	Becomes executive producer and cohost of *The View*
1998	Coanchors Sunday edition of *20/20* with colleague Diane Sawyer
1999	Interview with former White House intern Monica Lewinsky becomes one of the most-watched TV News events in history

Barrett, Mary Ellin. "Keeping Up with Barbara Walters." *Cosmopolitan*, June 1982.

Bumiller, Elisabeth. "So Famous, Such Clout, She Could Interview Herself." *New York Times*, 21 April 1996.

Davis, Gerry. *The Today Show: An Anecdotal History*. New York: William Morrow and Company, Inc., 1987.

Gerosa, Melina. "Who Fascinates Barbara Most?" *Ladies Home Journal*, April 1996.

Gunther, Marc. *The House that Roone Built: The Inside Story of ABC News*. Boston: Little, Brown and Company, 1994.

Hosley, David H. and Gayle K. Yamada, eds. *Hard News: The History of Women in Broadcasting*. New York: Greenwood Press, 1987.

Malone, Mary. *Barbara Walters: TV Superstar*. Hillside, NJ: Enslow, 1990.

Metz, Robert. *The Today Show*. Chicago: Playboy Press, 1977.

Oppenheimer, Jerry. *Barbara Walters: An Unauthorized Biography*. New York: St. Martin's Press, 1990.

Reagan, Ron. "Barbara Walters: She's Candid Off-Camera." *Ladies Home Journal*, June 1984.

Smith, Liz. "Barbara Walters." *Interview*, September 1984.

Walters, Barbara. "Barbara Walters: Two Decades at the Top." *TV Guide*, 27 April 1996.

INDEX

PICTURE CREDITS

Henna Remstein holds a B.A. in English from Temple University and a M.A. in Writing, Literature, and Publishing from Emerson College. A freelance writer, she was the contributing editor for several Chelsea House literary series titles, including *Asian-American Women Writers, British Women Fiction Writers, 1900–1960* (2 volumes), and *Henrik Ibsen*. She lives in Philadelphia, PA.

Matina S. Horner was president of Radcliffe College and associate professor of psychology and social relations at Harvard University. She is best known for her studies of women's motivation, achievement, and personality development. Dr. Horner has served on several national boards and advisory councils, including those of the National Science Foundation, Time Inc., and the Women's Research and Education Institute. She earned her B.A. from Bryn Mawr College and her Ph.D. from the University of Michigan, and holds honorary degrees from many colleges and universities, including Mount Holyoke, Smith, Tufts, and the University of Pennsylvania.